Images of America
Huntington Harbor Lighthouse

Pictured here in 1994 are, from left to right, Janis Mackey Harrington and Doug and Mary Harrington. Janis was responsible for starting the Save the Huntington Harbor Lighthouse Organization, a predecessor of the current organization, Huntington Lighthouse Preservation Society Inc. (Huntington Town Clerk's Archives.)

ON THE COVER: This is a 1945 picture of the Huntington Harbor Lighthouse in operation. In the far distance is the Lloyd Harbor Light Station, which burned down on November 12, 1947. (National Archives.)

IMAGES of America
HUNTINGTON HARBOR LIGHTHOUSE

Antonia S. Mattheou and Nancy Y. Moran
Foreword by Pamela Setchell
Introduction by Deanna Glassmann

ARCADIA
PUBLISHING

Copyright © 2020 by Antonia S. Mattheou and Nancy Y. Moran
ISBN 978-1-4671-0474-6

Published by Arcadia Publishing
Charleston, South Carolina

Library of Congress Control Number: 2019949897

For all general information, please contact Arcadia Publishing:
Telephone 843-853-2070
Fax 843-853-0044
E-mail sales@arcadiapublishing.com
For customer service and orders:
Toll-Free 1-888-313-2665

Visit us on the Internet at www.arcadiapublishing.com

To my daughter Diana Mattheou-Karras. You are the light in my life.

To my husband, Michael Moran. You have been to Antonia and me a sounding board, chauffeur, cook, and bartender while writing this book. We are grateful for your patience, support, understanding, and love! To my precious granddaughters Chloe and Mackenzie Moran, who inspire me and make my every day sunny.

Contents

Foreword		6
Acknowledgements		7
Introduction		8
1.	Lloyd Harbor Light Station	9
2.	Huntington Harbor Lighthouse	23
3.	Lightkeepers	49
4.	Huntington Harbor Lighthouse Restoration, 1985–2010	61
5.	Huntington Harbor Lighthouse Foundation Rehabilitation, 2011	77
6.	The Allure of Huntington Harbor	103

Foreword

It was a warm summer day in August when the Harrington family was sitting on the beach laughing while recapping their recent sailing trip to Huntington from Maine. I had the privilege and honor to be included on the trip for part of the way, enough of the excursion to feel it could become the story for another book.

The scenery along the Maine coast was spectacular when not encased in fog—and then somehow it still looks good in fog. Certainly, lighthouses look good in fog in more ways than one. Remember, this was one of the many reasons they were built. This was a celebration of the journey and the many lighthouses they saw; some they were very happy to see . . . or hear. And then, there it stood before them, their very own lighthouse offshore straight out in front of them—the Huntington Harbor Lighthouse. Or, at least, what was left of it.

Its windows were boarded up, and the cement showed the serious wear of many years of neglect. Little did they know that much of the roof was collapsed and the birds had, well, we can leave that to your imagination. It showed the remnants of what was once a grand structure of Beaux Arts style, much like a little castle. With all the lighthouses being cared for in Maine, how could we be so lucky to have our own and yet have left it in this horrid condition? Someone chimed in and mentioned that it was scheduled for demolition the following year. Oh, the horror! How could this happen? Who was responsible for it?

It was at that moment that chatter began within the family to make calls to point out the obvious. Surely, someone would jump in and stop it and begin to restore the interesting little structure. Little did they know it would be up to them to lead the charge. The daughter-in-law, Janis Mackey Harrington, thought she would take charge of spreading the word about the condition of the building. Her mother-in-law, Mary Harrington, exclaimed, "Oh Janis I'll help you, it would be such a nice summer project!"

And there it began in the summer of 1985!

—Pamela Setchell

ACKNOWLEDGMENTS

Presented between the covers of this book is what we hope to be an accurate, detailed history of two lighthouses in the town of Huntington. The original Lloyd Harbor Light Station was built in 1857 on a sand spit on the southeast point of Lloyd Neck and was destroyed by fire in 1947. A new structure was built in 1912 at the entrances of both Lloyd and Huntington Harbors, and it is now preserved as the oldest reinforced concrete lighthouse on the East Coast and the second oldest in the United States.

The making of this book would not have been possible without significant contributions and assistance from many dedicated and knowledgeable individuals who made this historical account more personal and accurate. Our sources for this book were manuscripts and images largely provided by the National Archives, the different yacht clubs in the town of Huntington, the Huntington Historical Society, the Huntington Lighthouse Archives, and the Huntington Town Clerk's Archives. We also had invaluable assistance from descendants of light keepers, such as Charles Burnham Jr., Evelyn M. Reilly, and Veronika Bleakley. We are only too glad to recognize the assistance offered by Karen Martin, archivist, Huntington Historical Society; Teresa Schwind, assistant director, Huntington Public Library; Joanne Kois, Head of the Bay Club; and Steven Eckers and Hank Bungart, board members of the Huntington Lighthouse Preservation Society.

We are indebted to Susan Glaser, Pamela Setchell, Torkel A. Knutson, Ethan Sands, Douglas Martines, Valerie Whyte, Stan Thomson, Pamela Griffin Hansen, John Almberg, Thaddeus Harden, Deanne Rathke (director of the Greenlawn-Centerport Historical Association), the US Coast Guard for providing images, and Thomas Hoffman for providing graphic enhancements. We owe special thanks to our contributors Henrietta Schavran, Oliver Bodine, Torkel A. Knutson, Judy Knutson Calabrese, Jackie Martin, Pamela Setchell, Nick De Santis, and especially Deanna Glassmann, who in addition to writing the introduction spent countless hours proofreading this manuscript.

We hope that you will take as much pleasure in reading and sharing this book with family and friends as we did in researching and writing it.

Introduction

Huntington Harbor Lighthouse, often referred to as the "Castle on the Bay," marks the entrance to two harbors: Huntington Harbor to the south and Lloyd Harbor to the west. This, however, was not always the case, as the history of the Huntington Harbor Lighthouse is the story of two lighthouses.

The first lighthouse, the Lloyd Harbor Light Station, was built and illuminated in 1857 to help sailing ships seek shelter. The Lloyd Harbor Light Station was manned by lighthouse keepers from its inception in November 1857 through June 16, 1912, when it was replaced by the second lighthouse, built in Huntington Harbor.

The construction of the Huntington Harbor Lighthouse, in a unique Beaux Arts style, began in 1910. It was the first poured reinforced concrete lighthouse built on the East Coast and was said to resemble a small castle.

On June 16, 1912, the Fresnel lens was removed from the Lloyd Harbor Light Station and relit in the Huntington Harbor Lighthouse at 7:42 p.m. The Huntington Harbor Lighthouse stands 48 feet high, which is 42 feet above the high-water mark.

The duties of the lighthouse keeper kept him busy from sunup to sundown and often throughout the night. His primary responsibility was to keep the light shining at night and the foghorn signaling in foggy weather. Entries were made into a daily log noting work done at the lighthouse, weather and water conditions, and any other activity that took place that day. Additionally, all the housekeeping chores were carried out by the keeper, including all maintenance of the lighthouse structure and the lighthouse boat. The premises were periodically inspected by an official inspector.

For 36 years, the Huntington Harbor Lighthouse housed members of the US Lighthouse Service and subsequently the US Coast Guard. However, in 1948, the lighthouse was automated and no longer needed a keeper. The workings of the lighthouse were then controlled by the Eatons Neck Light Station. While the Coast Guard took care of the lens and the foghorn, it paid no attention to the structure itself. Ultimately, this unique lighthouse structure slipped into disrepair. In 1984, the federal government decided to demolish the lighthouse and erect a steel tower with a light atop it in its place. Cries of protest emerged from concerned boaters, shipping interests, and local inhabitants. Consequently, in 1985, the government relented and leased the lighthouse to the Save Huntington Lighthouse Organization, whose stated goal was to save and restore the lighthouse to its original grandeur. Eighteen years later, in 2003, after painstaking work by many volunteers, the Huntington Harbor Lighthouse was deemed saved and was open to visitors. The organization was renamed the Huntington Lighthouse Preservation Society in 2007. Preservation projects are continuous due to the harsh environment surrounding this offshore lighthouse. Windows and doors have been repaired, and walls have been plastered again and again. However, the most far-reaching preservation project was the two-year restoration of the underwater concrete foundation, an amazing feat of engineering.

It is the mission of the Huntington Lighthouse Preservation Society to continue to preserve and maintain this unique structure, an important part of the history of Huntington, New York. We hope that you enjoy this story of our two lighthouses from inception, through change, towards possible demolition, and finally on to preservation. Come take a ride with us!

—Deanna Glassmann

One
LLOYD HARBOR
LIGHT STATION

The original light station structure was built in 1857 on a sand spit. Built of wood and brick, the lightkeeper's dwelling was one and a half stories high with a shingled roof. It consisted of one sitting room, three bedrooms, and a kitchen. Rainwater was collected in a 5,000-gallon cistern constructed of brick and lined with cement. The water was purified using lime and charcoal. (National Archives.)

As early as November 22, 1838, Lt. George M. Bache proposed that a light must be placed in Lloyd Harbor at the end of East Beach. Again, on August 9, 1853, Hiram Paulding, at the request of "the watermen" navigating on Long Island Sound, recommended to James Guthrie, US secretary of the treasury, that a beacon be erected in Lloyd Harbor. He felt that in stormy weather, Lloyd Harbor was the only refuge for many miles for vessels navigating the sound. Paulding, a US Navy captain, was stationed at the Washington, DC, Navy Yard at the time. After the Civil War, he made Huntington his residence. (National Archives.)

By an act of Congress on August 3, 1854, the amount of $4,000 was appropriated for the construction of a beacon light to mark the entrance to Lloyd Harbor. Additionally, in 1873, the amount of $2,000 was also approved to build a seawall made of large rocks in order to protect the lighthouse structure from the abrasion of the sea waves. (National Archives.)

An Act

Ceding jurisdiction to the United States over lands to be occupied as sites of light houses and keepers' dwellings within this State.

Passed January 24, 1855.

The People of the State of New York represented in Senate and Assembly, do enact as follows:

Section 1. Jurisdiction is hereby ceded to the United States over so much land as may be necessary for the construction and maintenance of light houses and keepers' dwellings, within this State, as

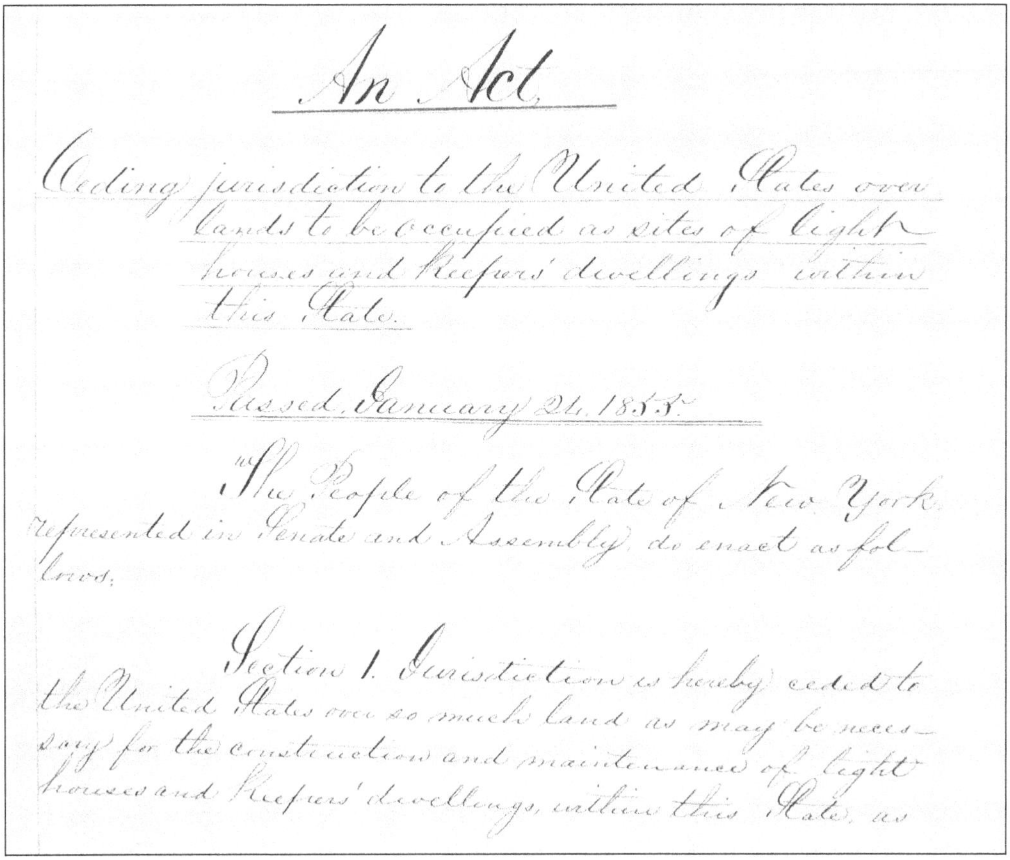

In an act dated January 24, 1855, the State of New York ceded jurisdiction to the United States over lands for the necessary construction and maintenance of lighthouses and keepers' dwellings within the state. (National Archives.)

Lloyd's Harbor Light

Saml Denton

and Wife

TO

United States

of America

DEED.

Dated July 24th 1855

Light House Board

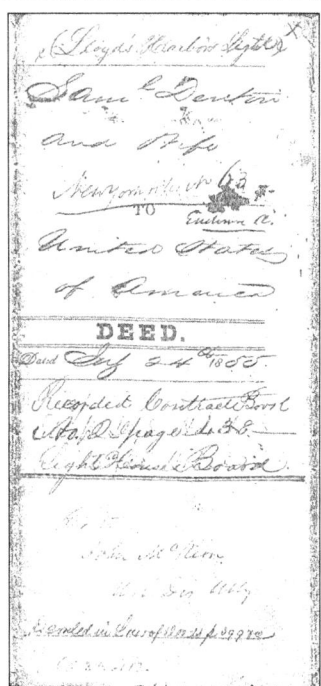

On July 24, 1855, the federal government purchased two and a half acres of land for $250 from Samuel Denton on the southeast point of Lloyd Neck for the purpose of constructing a light station. With time, the area was reduced greatly by the sea. The deed was recorded in Contract Book No. 2 of the Lighthouse Board and at Oyster Bay, Queens County, New York. (National Archives.)

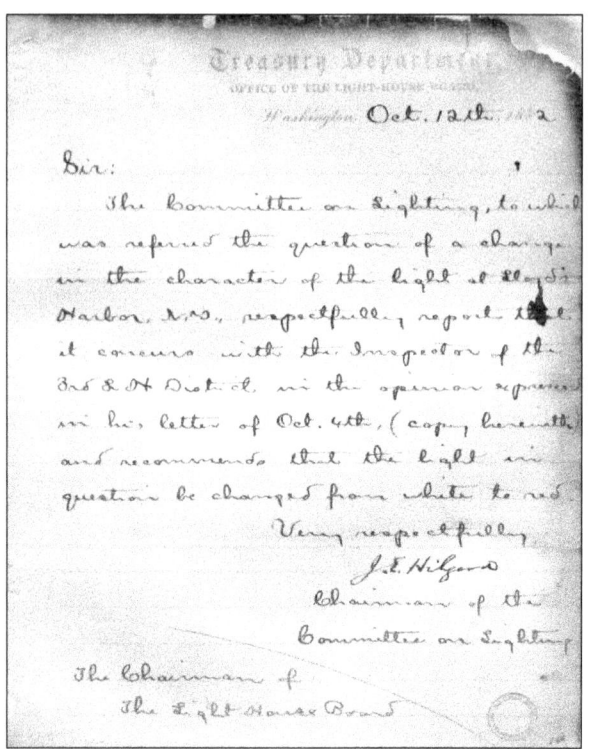

The original character of the light apparatus was a fixed, white, fifth-order Henry-Lepaute Fresnel lens. There were four panels in the lens, with five prisms above the central belt and three below. The structure surrounding the lens, called the lantern, was of the fourth order. The lower section of the lantern was made of iron lined with wood, and the lantern had an iron roof. The lightning conductor was also made of iron. On October 12, 1882, the character of the light apparatus changed to red. (National Archives.)

The cost to build a brick tower with a beam light was $2,929. The whitewashed tower was connected to the keeper's dwelling on one corner, with a wooden stairway through a passageway on the second story. It had two landings consisting of two stairs each, one window at the top, and one door at the base. The shape of the tower was square. Its interior base diameter measured seven feet, and its height from the base to the focal plane of the lantern was 34 feet. (National Archives.)

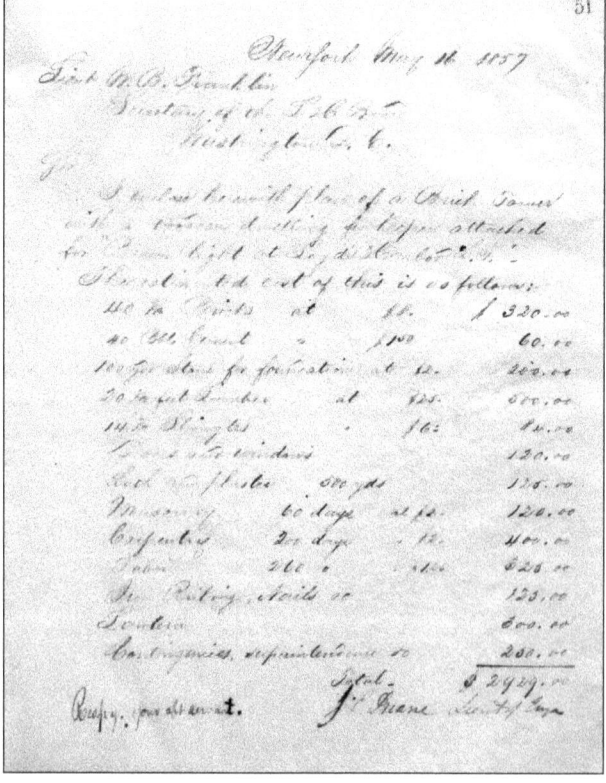

The assembly of the station's frame commenced on August 3, 1857, at Deep River by master carpenter Mr. Dennison and his four workers. Dennison received $2.25 and the other carpenters $1.75 per day each for the work performed. Timber for the bell tower was ordered and was to be shipped to Lloyd Neck after the station's framing was completed and delivered to Lloyd Harbor by Stevens & Starkey. (National Archives.)

Here is the light station as seen in 1884 from the deck of the yacht *Ella*. In 1867, a shed for fuel was added along with a small cellar under the east room where the oil for the lamp was kept in one 100-gallon and one 50-gallon oil butt on a wooden stand. A new lantern room and iron railing were also added to the structure. A chicken coop, woodshed, and outhouse are also visible. (Huntington Historical Society.)

This approved contract was sent by engineer secretary Peter C. Haius to Col. I.C. Woodruff, engineer of the Third Lighthouse District, New York, for a jetty to be built at the light station for the purpose of protecting the site. Unfortunately, the jetty built did not offer the protection needed, and by 1873, more money was appropriated for the construction of a stone wall. This project was finished in 1875. (National Archives.)

A survey of the Lloyd Harbor Light Station was performed by A.F. Jentys on September 19, 1895. It indicated the footprints of the buildings and included the following information: the latitude of the tower was 40° 54' 54" north and longitude 73° 26' 06" west; the height of the focal plane of the lantern above mean sea level was 40 feet; and the base of the tower above the water mark was about six feet. The purpose of the light was to guide ships in the bay and harbor. The light station could be accessed from the beach as well as from the land. (Huntington Town Clerk's Archives.)

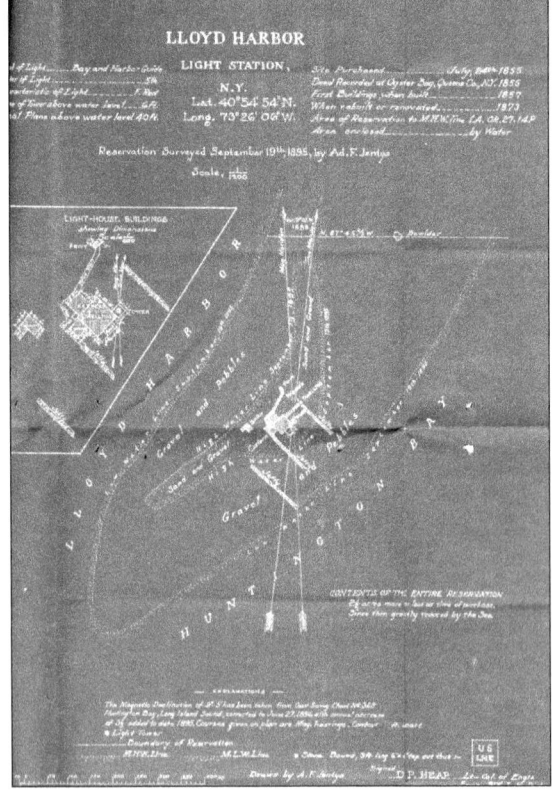

On June 16, 1892, the US Treasury Office of the Lighthouse Board approved Edward R. Lowe's bid of $1,500 to build the east breakwater wall higher in order to protect the foundation of the lighthouse tower and dwelling from encroachment by the sea. The original bid submitted by Lowe was for $1,000. Realizing that he made a mistake, he resubmitted his bid for $1,500, which was still the lowest bid received for the job. The breakwater wall was completed in 1893. Under the same contract, the underpinning under the southwest corner of the dwelling was also rebuilt. In 1898, two hundred tons of riprap were added to the breakwater. (National Archives.)

The purchase of the 200 tons of riprap added to the breakwater wall of the light station was approved in 1897. (National Archives.)

By 1895, the lighthouse structure was altered again, as seen in these two images. The keeper's dwelling was overhauled and repaired. The porch's platform was rebuilt and floored, and the chimney on the dwelling was rebuilt from the roof. The building was now a two-story structure with 11 rooms, including an attic, all on a deeply laid foundation of brick. The light tower remained unchanged and was still attached to the keeper's quarters. (Above, Steve Eckers; below, National Archives.)

According to a report by an inspector from the US Department of Commerce and Labor, the property of the light station was deemed very valuable based on the gravel found in the area, and it was decided not to sell. There were other reasons as well. Since the living quarters at the proposed new lighthouse site were not sufficient for a keeper with a family, permitting the keeper to reside at the old light station structure was a good alternative. That also saved the expense of a caretaker for the old light station, which would have been required if the keeper did not live there. (National Archives.)

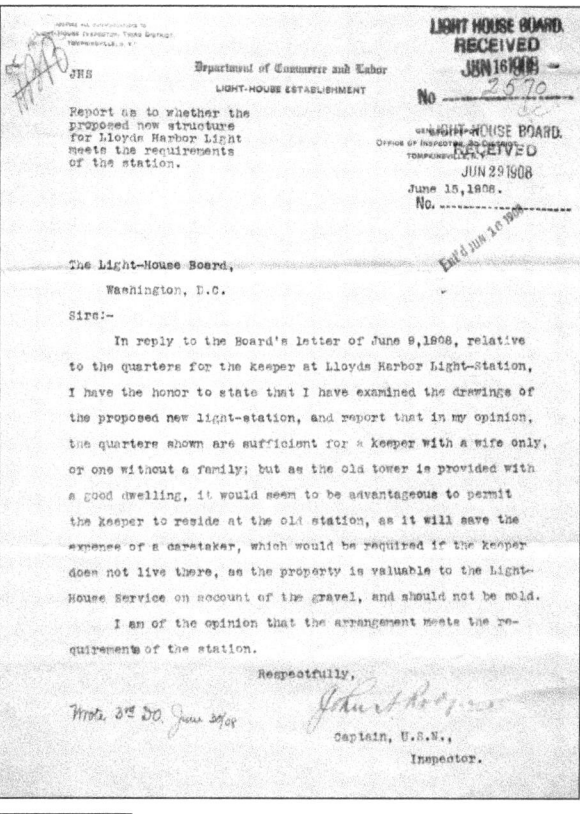

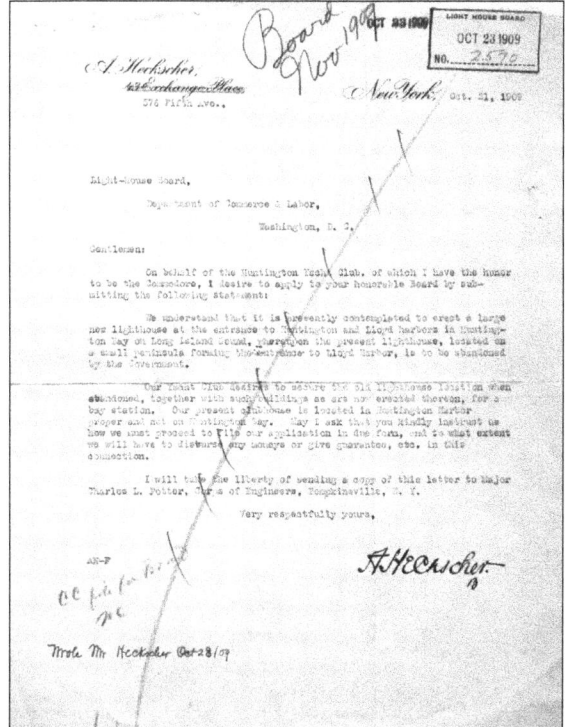

On October 23, 1909, August Heckscher, as commodore of the Huntington Yacht Club, requested from the Department of Commerce and Labor in Washington, DC, the use of the Lloyd Harbor Light Station with all the buildings, as soon as they were abandoned, as a bay station for the club. (National Archives.)

Lightkeeper Robert McGlone had five children—three daughters and two sons. On March 24, 1900, when their mother, Margaret Spring McGlone, died, Augusta Harrigan was hired to take care of them. The McGlone children continued to live in the Lloyd Harbor Light Station with Augusta Harrigan even after 1912, while their father continued serving as the keeper at the Huntington Harbor Lighthouse. (Huntington Town Clerk's Archives.)

This page from the 1909 log indicates complaints pertaining to the keeper's son, who used the lighthouse boat, and to the keeper for having a sandworm and clam business. The keeper responded that it was his son who got the sandworms and clams. Robert McGlone was serving as the keeper of the lighthouse. The person of interest was one of his two sons, the older son being 23 and the younger 16 years of age. (National Archives.)

There were many inquiries regarding the renting or purchasing of the Lloyd Harbor Light Station reservation lands. On May 14, 1924, Walter Drake, assistant secretary of commerce, requested from Robert L. Bacon in the US House of Representatives to use the light station as well as a portion of the Fire Island Lighthouse as residences for disabled war veterans. In 1936, the Motion Picture Corporation of America also submitted a bid to the Town of Huntington for the purchase of the reservation. (National Archives.)

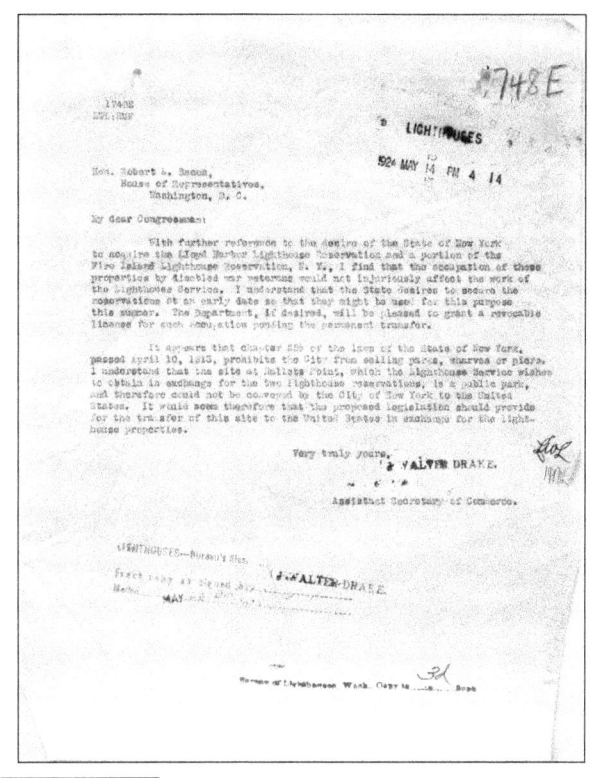

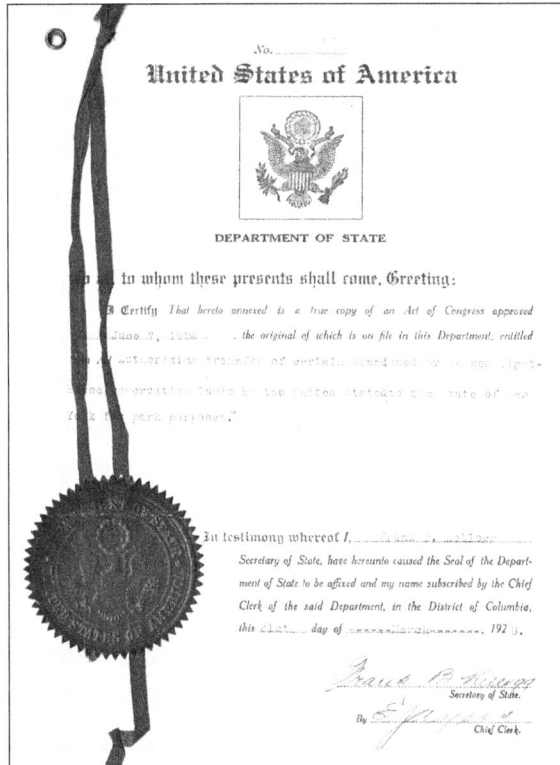

On June 7, 1924, the Unites States deeded the lighthouse reservation lands to the State of New York for park purposes. As of June 1, 1928, under commissioner of lighthouses G.R. Putnam, the land and buildings known as Lloyd Harbor Light Station were granted to the Town of Huntington for public park purposes. Today, nature lovers and canoe and kayak users enjoy the serenity that this spot offers. (Huntington Town Clerk's Archives.)

This photograph of the light station in 1935, from the collection of Evelyn Reilly, was taken while her grandfather Michael Fish was serving as caretaker. Her father, Arthur Hubbs, and his brother Raymond were house painters in Huntington. Her father was also a volunteer fireman and played clarinet in one of the town's fire departments' bands. (Evelyn Reilly.)

This image of the Lloyd Harbor Light Station shows where Evelyn Reilly spent time as a young child during many summers in the mid-1930s. Her uncles Stewart Holden (left) and Joe McDonald are seen standing on the porch. She remembers, "There was no electricity, water was pumped from a well—and, of course the outhouse. But as children none of that mattered!" (Evelyn Reilly.)

On November 12, 1947, the light station was destroyed by fire during a gale. Only the chimney of the house and the watch tower remained. Authorities believed that duck hunters had stayed at the abandoned light station the night before and a cigarette ignited the rubbish lying around. The keeper of the new lighthouse, Richard J. White, recorded that the old light station had burned down. At right is a page of his log where he also noted that the tide was very high that day. (Above, Huntington Town Clerk's Archives; right, National Archives.)

These are two recent images of the Lloyd Harbor Light Station site. Those sailing near the spit of land where the station stood can still see a few blocks here and there, remnants of the chimney, the original metal cupola, the base of the tower, and the old jetty. They are reminders of the light station that stood there in bygone days. (Both, Deanna Glassmann.)

Two

Huntington Harbor Lighthouse

This lighthouse was built at the entrance of Lloyd and Huntington Harbors on a quarter-acre of wharf three miles offshore. The boat landing was built at one corner of the pier on the south side of the lighthouse. In his December 29, 1912, report, inspector Oscar C. Luther described the lighthouse as having a submarine site, a tower in the front, and two rooms. (National Archives.)

Interest in replacing the Lloyd Harbor Light Station is indicated by this 1883 letter from J.L. Davis, chairman of the US Treasury Department's Committee of Location of the Lighthouse Board in Washington, DC. Davis was referring to a petition filed "by those navigating the Long Island Sound" who were interested in establishing a new lighthouse at Lloyd Harbor, Huntington. (National Archives.)

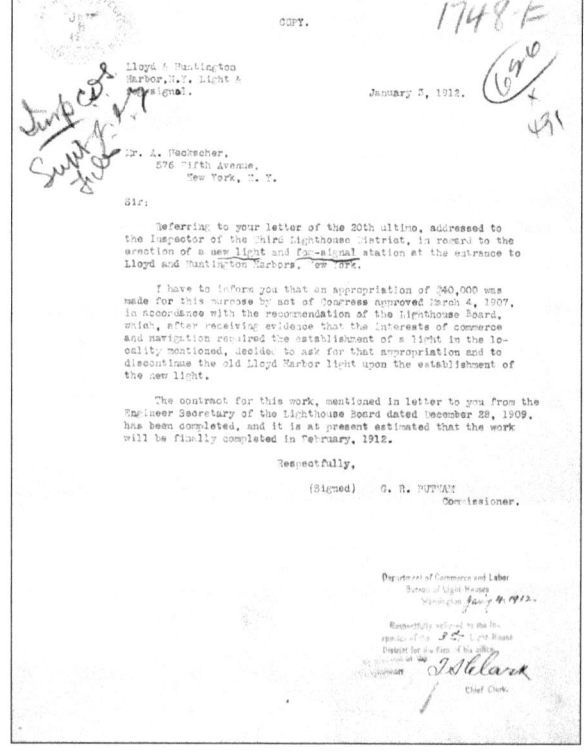

A response to Huntington resident August Heckscher from Commissioner G.R. Putman informs him that Congress approved a $40,000 appropriation on March 4, 1907, for the establishment of a new lighthouse at the entrance to Lloyd and Huntington Harbors. The decision was made based on evidence that the interest of commerce and navigation required the establishment of a lighthouse in the area. (National Archives.)

On March 4, 1907, the federal government appropriated $40,000 for the construction of a new lighthouse in Huntington Harbor. According to the document received by the Lighthouse Board in June 1908, the total estimated cost to build the new lighthouse structure, install the fog signal, lantern, and riprap, and purchase other building necessities totaled $34,000. (National Archives.)

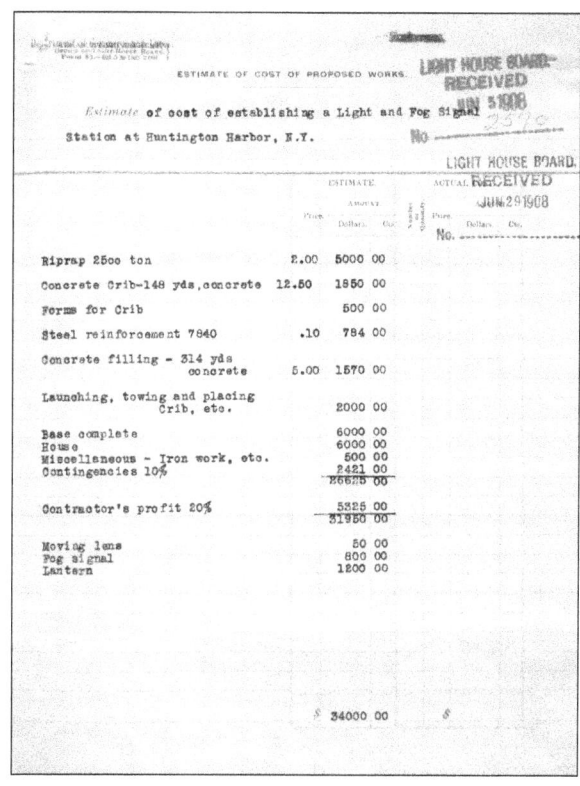

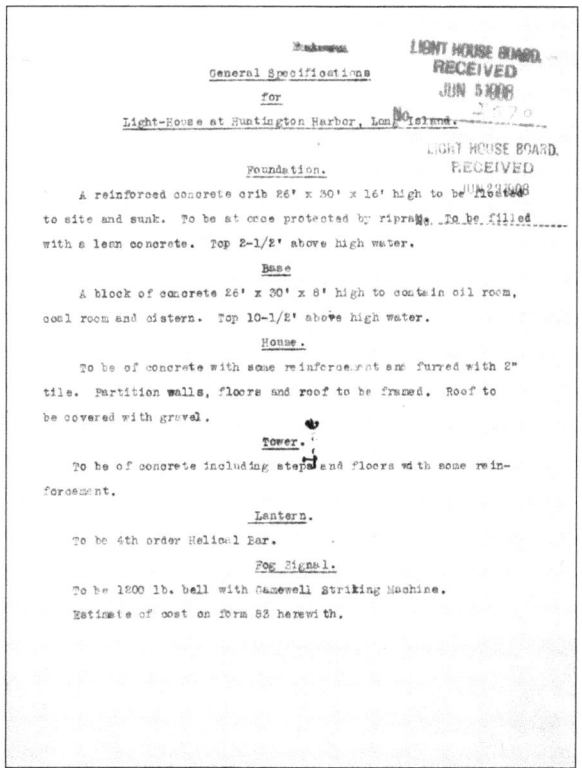

The lighthouse was built of concrete from the foundation to the tower and had a fourth-order helical bar lantern. The foundation crib measured 26 by 30 by 16 feet, stood 2½ feet above high water, and was protected by riprap; the base measured 26 by 30 by 8 feet and stood 10½ feet above high water. The interior was reinforced and furred with 2-inch tile, and the roof was covered with gravel. (National Archives.)

In his remarks to the Lighthouse Board on June 18, 1908, the engineer secretary admitted that a concrete crib was a new idea in lighthouse practice. Additionally, he suggested that the bottom of the crib should penetrate the shoal about two feet rather than rest directly on top for the reason that settlement was less likely to occur. (National Archives.)

A letter from the Department of Commerce and Labor was sent to the Lighthouse Board of the Third Lighthouse District on October 5, 1909, requesting approval of the contract between the United States and the firm of Charles Meads & Company to build the new Huntington Harbor Lighthouse. The contract was for $27,170. (National Archives.)

> **THE WESTERN UNION TELEGRAPH COMPANY**
> 25,000 OFFICES IN AMERICA CABLE SERVICE TO ALL THE WORLD
> ROBERT C. CLOWRY, PRESIDENT   BELVIDERE BROOKS, GENERAL MANAGER
>
> Huntington N.Y. Sept 28 1910
>
> To Lighthouse Inspector
> Tompkinsville N.Y.
>
> Crib drawing fourteen feet water barred from staked site by ledge with twelve feet water over. Unless otherwise ordered, will place crib eighty feet northeast at six tonight. Assistant Inspector Hayward here concurs.
>
> Gov't rates. Official — Collect — Dillenbeck

On September 28, 1910, at 6:00 p.m., the lighthouse inspector was informed that the crib of the lighthouse in Huntington Harbor was to be placed 80 feet northeast of the proposed site; assistant inspector George M. Hayward concurred. A day later, as stated in the telegram below, the Bureau of Lighthouses granted permission to the lighthouse inspector to relocate the foundation of the lighthouse to its present site at latitude 40° 54' 42" north and longitude 73° 25' 52" west. (Both, National Archives.)

> OFFICIAL BUSINESS   AVC-WHM   TELEGRAM   GOVERNMENT RATES
> FROM 99-
>   Department of Commerce and Labor
> Bureau of Light-Houses
> (BUREAU OR OFFICE)
>   Washington,
>   September 29, 1910.
>
> Lighthouse Inspector,
>   Saint George, New York.
>
> Authority granted to locate Lloyds Harbor new light from sixty to eighty feet northeast of proposed site in accordance request by telephone
>
>   PUTNAM.
>
> CONFIRMATION   Commissioner.
>
> CHARGE DEPARTMENT OF COMMERCE AND LABOR, APPROPRIATION FOR Supplies of Light-Houses

An attempt was made on Friday, September 23, 1910, to launch the caisson, but it became wedged, and it was necessary to get a tug from New London to haul it off. Finally, on Saturday, October 1, it was lowered into position by allowing water into its compartments. The water was then pumped out, and the compartments were filled with concrete. The new lighthouse structure was two stories above the foundation, and the light tower was added to the structure. (National Archives.)

The caisson was built at Lloyd Neck on government property near the site of the old Lloyd Harbor Light Station. On October 10, 1910, the *Brooklyn Eagle* reported that the lighthouse caisson at Huntington Inlet weighed 300 tons, measured 30 feet square, was 16 feet high, and was divided by partitions into four sections. Each partition was 13 inches thick. The prospective plan was that the lighthouse would be completed "before rough weather comes." (National Archives.)

On October 10, 1910, the American Federation of Labor Compressed Air & Foundation Workers' Union sent a letter to the New York State Lighthouse Department requesting more particulars as to the construction of the new Huntington Harbor Lighthouse. Also pictured is a newspaper clipping announcing the towing of the lighthouse caisson into position. (National Archives.)

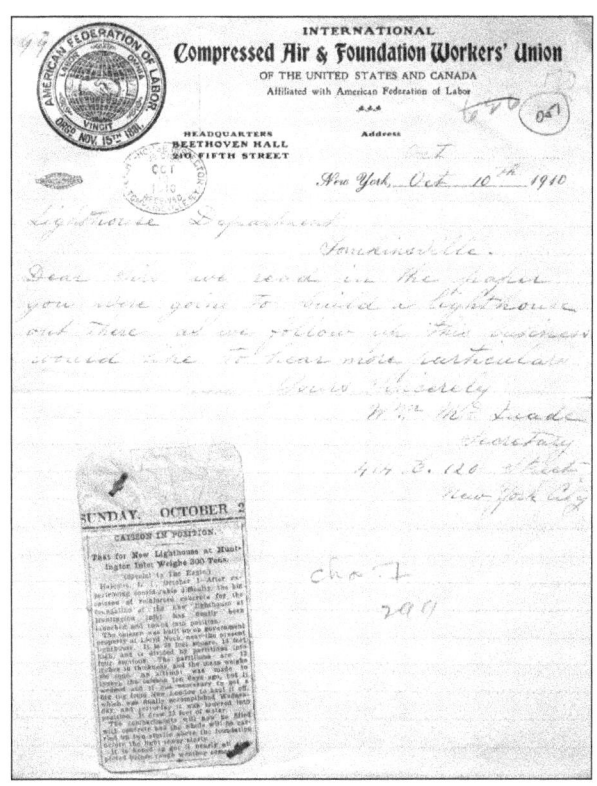

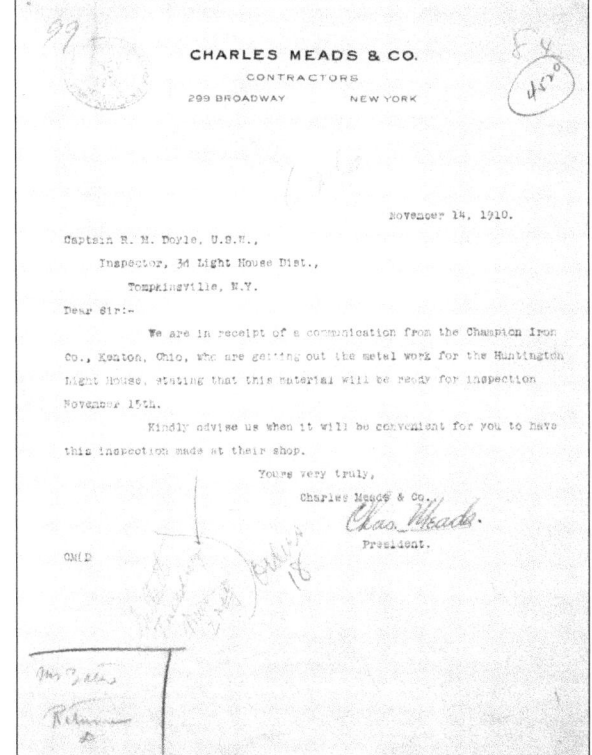

Charles Meads, president of the contractor Charles Meads & Company, sent a letter dated November 14, 1910, informing Capt. R.M. Doyle, US Navy, inspector of the Third Lighthouse District, that the metal work produced for the Huntington Harbor Lighthouse by the Champion Iron Company of Kenton, Ohio, would be ready for inspection on November 15. (National Archives.)

The Carnegie Steel Company supplied the structural steel for the lighthouse. The beam pictured here is located on the left side of the staircase leading to the watch deck. The marking "09" indicates that the steel beam was manufactured in 1909. The name Roebling Iron Works has been noted on other beams; the same Brooklyn plant supplied the steel for the Brooklyn Bridge. (Pam Setchell, Viewpoint Photography.)

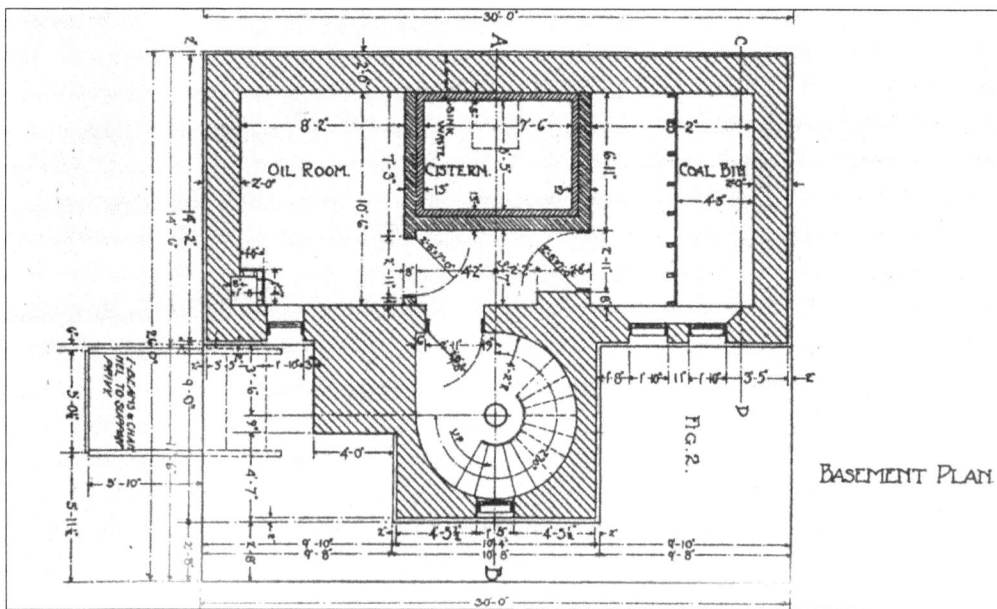

An original blueprint of the lighthouse shows that the basement consisted of an oil room, a coal room, and a brick cistern for freshwater storage. Rainwater of good quality was gathered in the 2,000-gallon cistern to last the whole year. A hand pump in the kitchen sink was used to obtain water from the basement. A dumbwaiter was used to bring oil, kerosene, and coal to the kitchen. Today, the basement houses a marine bathroom and storage areas. (National Archives.)

A report from Joseph T. Yates, superintendent of the Lighthouse Service, indicated that the installation of a flushing closet in the basement and discontinuance of the outside privy would be less of a distraction from the appearance of the station. An extension of the skeleton boat landing would also be needed over the riprap for a smoother landing. Yates noted that the area would be better served by the building of two small acetylene beacons onshore; in addition, using the old station as the keeper's living quarters would be inconvenient during the winter months due to the drifting ice. (National Archives.)

Lightkeeper Robert McGlone received the keys to the Huntington Harbor Lighthouse from Commander C.D. Stearns, the US Navy inspector, in December 1911. (National Archives.)

This picture of the lighthouse shows the outdoor privy that was installed in December 1912, according to lighthouse inspector Oscar C. Luther. It was mounted on a set of stilts attached to the east side of the lighthouse. An indoor toilet was installed in the basement in 1928, when indoor plumbing became available. (National Archives.)

This closeup image of the entrance area shows where the landing was located in the 1930s. In earlier years, this was where the wooden privy stood. The metal bars that were part of the base can still be seen. The Huntington Harbor Lighthouse is the oldest reinforced concrete lighthouse on the East Coast and the second oldest in the United States. (Antonia S. Mattheou.)

The handwritten note at right indicates plans to remove the wooden privy and use it as a storehouse. The vacant area was to be made into a platform protected by railing. The plan allowed for stairs to be built that would lead from the platform to the riprap. Below, A.N. Saxton, the engineer in charge of the construction work by Charles Meads & Company, suggested the removal of the privy from the exterior as well because it spoiled the architectural effect attempted in the design of the lighthouse. The privy was then to be moved to the basement between the coal bin and cistern by drilling outlets through the wall for discharge and saltwater inlet. A small hand pump was to be attached to flush the toilet. (Both, National Archives.)

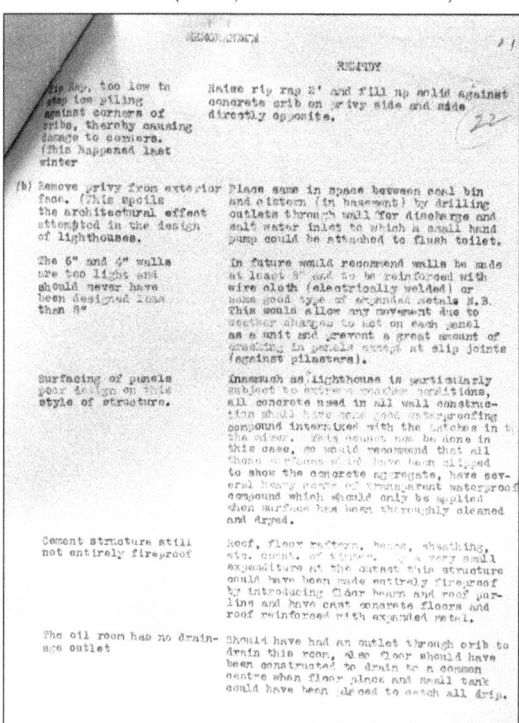

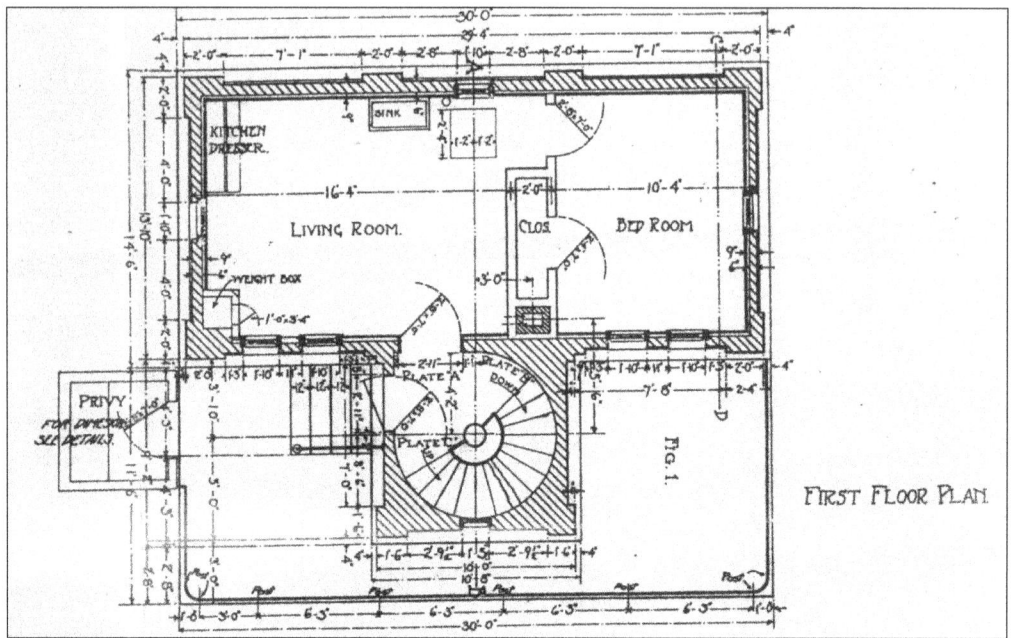

This blueprint shows the main entrance of the lighthouse, which leads to the first floor, consisting of a kitchen/living room and a bedroom. The amenities were very basic. The kitchen was equipped with a stove, a 34-by-16-by-6-inch sink, and a size 2 pump. The hand pump was used to obtain water from the cistern in the basement. Heat during the winter was provided by a potbelly coal stove. The stove was also used for cooking and keeping coffee warm. During the summer, the windows were kept open for cooling. (National Archives.)

This door, on the east side of the structure, was the only way the lightkeeper could get onto the lighthouse landing during the early years of operation. The door still exists today but is not being used. (Antonia S. Mattheou.)

This chart points out the location of the 1857 Lloyd Harbor Light Station at East Beach in Lloyd Neck and the piles of the proposed site of the 1912 lighthouse. Many boat captains welcomed the news of a new lighthouse that would serve both Huntington and Lloyd Harbors, as their boats had many times been grounded on the rocks while entering Huntington Harbor. (National Archives.)

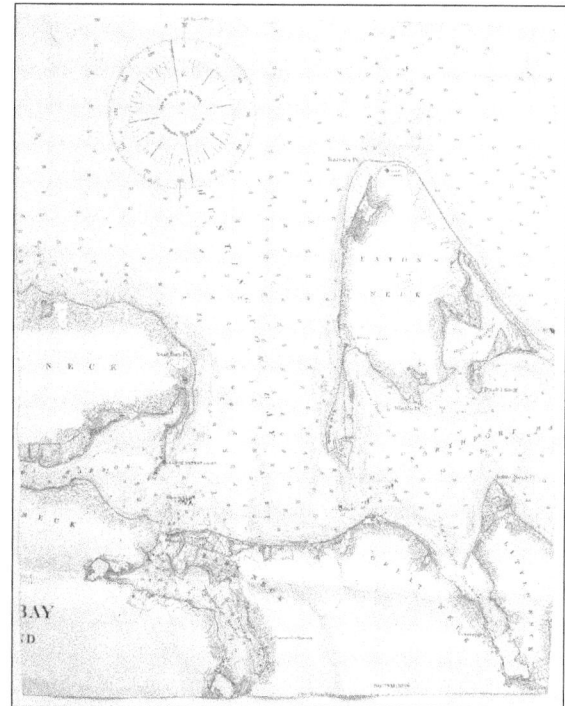

The lighthouse walls are constructed of four layers. The outer layer is of cement. The basic wall is made of poured concrete. Attached to it is a red clay terra-cotta tile covered with a scratch coat of cement. Finally, the inside coat is of plaster or stucco. The interior of the lighthouse is painted a seafoam green, as it has always been. (Huntington Lighthouse Archives.)

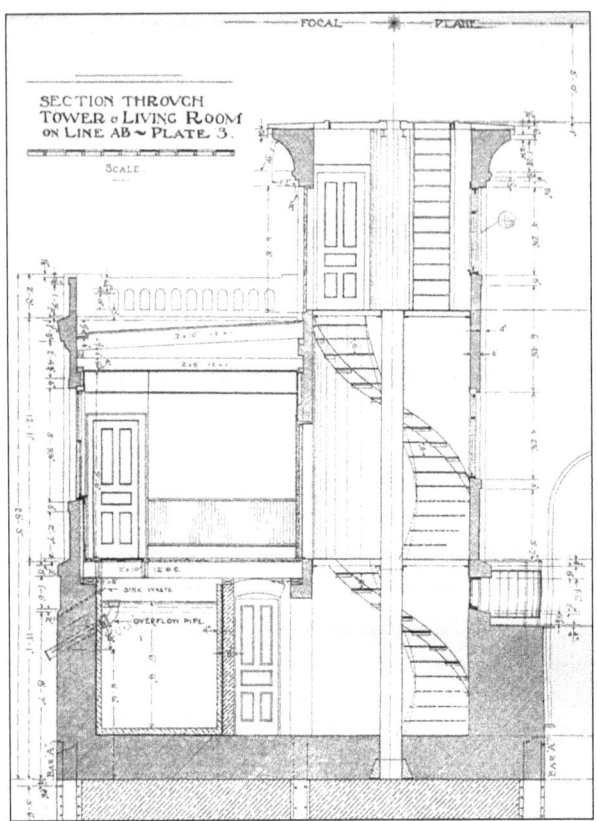

This blueprint depicts the circular cast iron stairway that leads from the basement to the living room and watch deck areas. The stairway is attached to an iron column that housed the lighthouse fog bell system. This system had a weight-and-pulley escapement that utilized weights to start a time session. Over the years, the weights have rusted in place. (National Archives.)

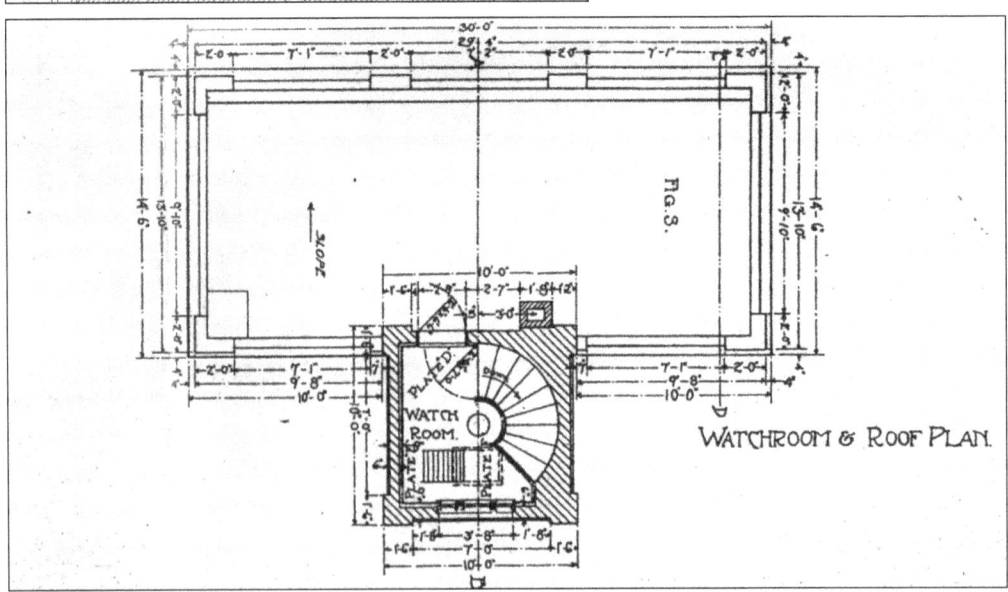

An iron ladder leads to the lantern and watch room. The door leading into this room is an iron trap fitted with hinges and bolts. It was the keeper's responsibility to keep the lantern brightly shining and the burner filled. At night, the keeper had to make several trips up and down the ladder to ensure the light had not gone out. A well-fitted cast iron door with a well-made brass latch leads to the outside deck of the lantern room. (National Archives.)

The lantern room is surmounted by an octagonal glass room composed of eight castings connected to each other by thirty-two 5/8-inch rough bolts. A hood neatly fitted above the castings has ventilator openings that can be closed from the inside with brass disks. Tower windows were storm windows with buff Holland shades on spring rollers to shade the entire length of the window, furnished with solid supports, best-quality cord, and two nickel-plated pulling rings. Red panels were added to the southernmost windows to warn mariners of the rocky shoal of the West Bank of Huntington Harbor. Today, the hooks remain above the corners of the windows. Below, a letter from keeper McGlone dated September 6, 1912, requests curtains for the windows 3 feet, 3 inches long and 2 feet, 8½ inches wide. The early glass had a tendency to acquire a faint green tint with continuous exposure to direct sunlight. This coloration of the prisms, although ever so slight, affected the amount of light a lens would put out. (Above, Ethan Sands; below, National Archives.)

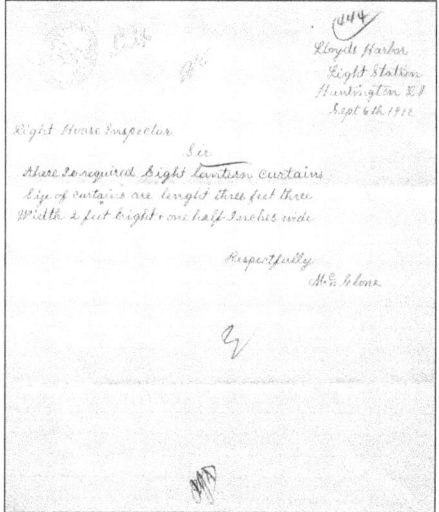

This closeup image of the lighthouse's southeast side was possibly taken before curtains were installed in the lantern room. Notice the fog bell on the lantern deck and the iron stovepipe extending from the west face of the lighthouse. The keeper's boat is resting on the landing. At that time, the landing was built on square columns made of cement. (US Coast Guard.)

On January 11, 1912, the estimated cost for improvements to the lighthouse amounted to $4,777. That included the purchase of 800 tons of riprap to raise the existing wall around the lighthouse and to fill in the boat landing, 600 tons of quarry stone to be used to caulk the riprap, two No. 4 Gamewell fog bell striking machines (one spare), one fog bell (1,000 pounds), building a new boat landing and resetting the boat davits, shifting the lens from the old to the new lighthouse, and removing the outside privy and building one in the basement. (National Archives.)

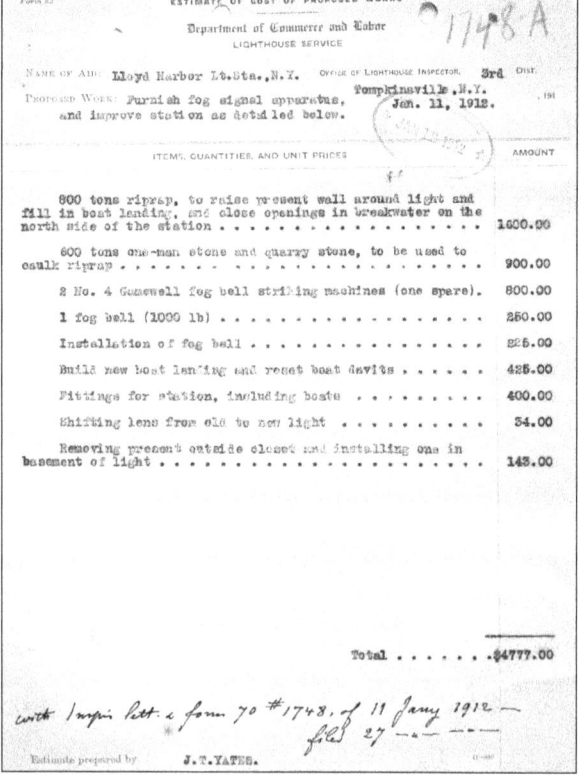

The original lighthouse plan called for a fourth-order helical bar. The lantern had eight sides, all glazed, with vertical bars and was constructed of iron. The original glass fifth-order Henry-Lepaute Fresnel lens was about 22 inches tall and 15 inches in diameter, weighed 400 pounds, and flashed in 345 degrees. When the light was in proper working order, it could be seen from seven to nine miles away. Eventually, the Fresnel lens was replaced by the Coast Guard with economical plastic lenses and later with a 300-millimeter optic, with a white light flashing every six seconds—three seconds on and three seconds off. As shown below, the 300-millimeter optic has been replaced by an LED light. However, the focal plane of the light is still 42 feet above the high water mark. (Both, Pam Setchell, Viewpoint Photography.)

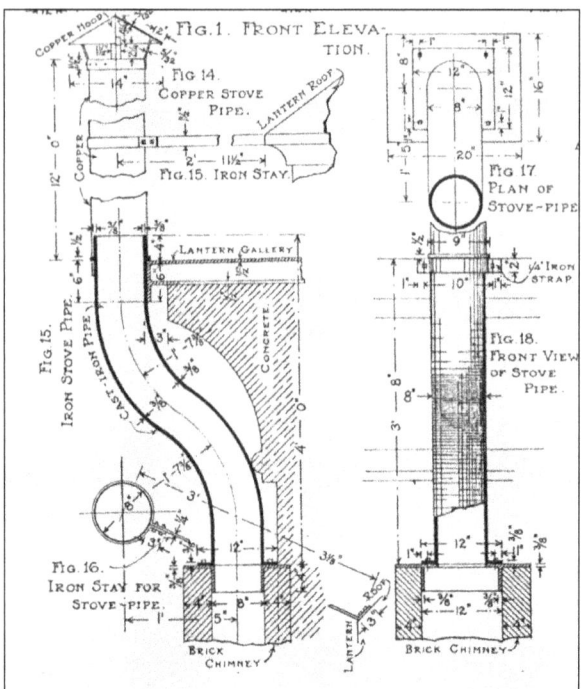

This plate, part of the original prints of the lighthouse, shows the brick chimney that housed the cast iron stovepipe, which to this day can be seen on the watch deck. The pipe hood and the portion of the pipe that extended 12 feet from the base of the lantern gallery were made of copper. (National Archives.)

The discontinuation of the Lloyd Harbor Light Station and the initiation of the new lighthouse were announced in the publication *Notice to Mariners*. The new lighthouse had a fixed red light with a fifth-order lens that had the intensity of 90 English candles and was elevated 42 feet above water. The structure was a one-story concrete dwelling of natural color resting on a rectangular pier. (National Archives.)

In preparation of initiating the new lighthouse, machinist Barney Murphy wrote a letter to the inspector of the Third Lighthouse District on June 20, 1912. He informed the inspector that he removed the lens pedestal and protector from the Lloyd Harbor Light Station on June 15, set it on the new lighthouse, and turned it on to try it. He also connected more chain to the Gamewell bell striker on the lantern deck of the new lighthouse. Below, in a note dated June 16, 1912, keeper Robert McGlone reported to the lighthouse inspector that he "started the light in the new Lighthouse at 7:32 pm and everything was working fine." (Both, National Archives.)

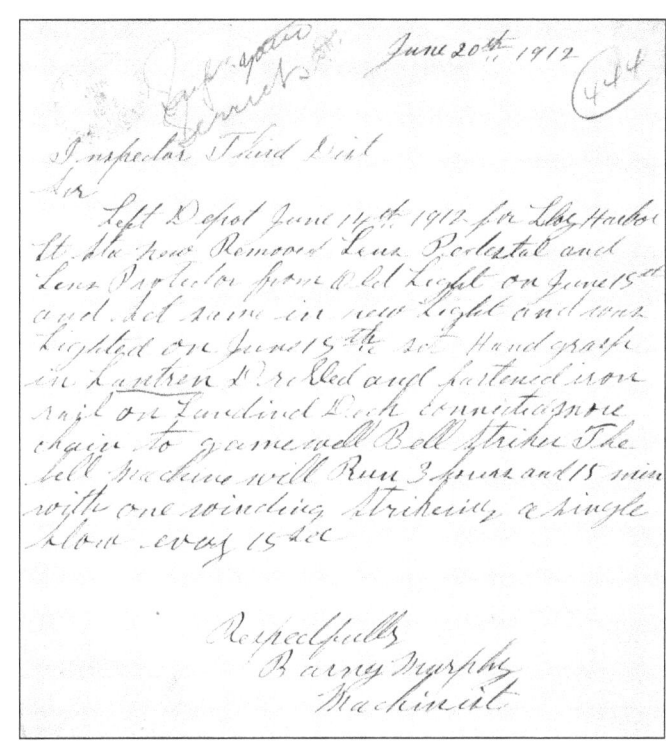

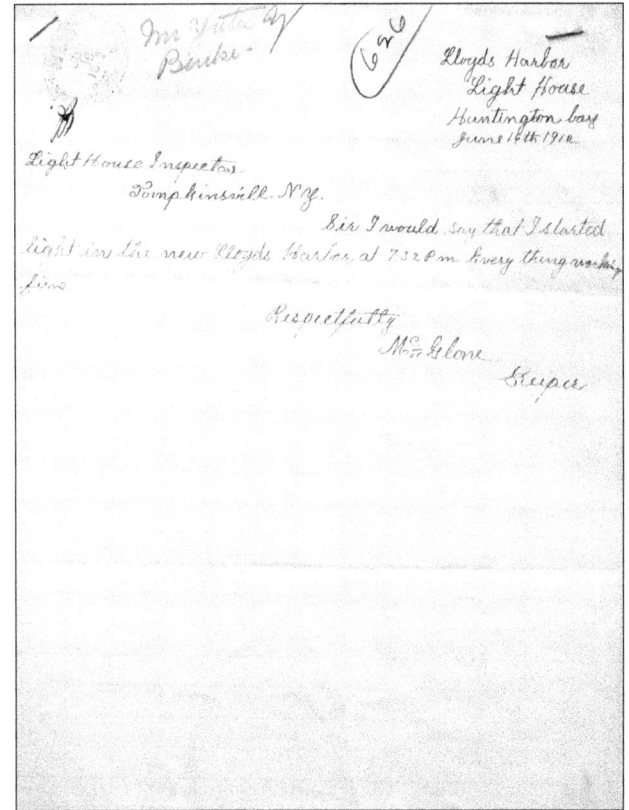

On June 16, 1912, the day the lighthouse started operation, the lightkeeper recorded in his log the forecast of the day. He wrote that there was a light south wind blowing at first and it was partly cloudy. Later it became partly foggy. (National Archives.)

This 1936 image shows curtains installed in the lantern room to prevent the sun from heating the glass prisms that made up the Fresnel lens. When sun heated the prisms, the glass pieces expanded. The prisms were trapped within a brass framework, with no place for them to go. A snug fit within the brass frame caused them to chip, or in extreme cases, shatter when they expanded. Prisms not tightly mounted within the frame caused the litharge—a lead-based putty—to be forced out of place. This loosened the prisms, which could fall out of the frame. (National Archives.)

In 1912, the bell on the Huntington Harbor Lighthouse was installed on the lantern deck on the channel side. It was manufactured in Jersey City, New Jersey, in 1911, had a Gamewell Model No. 4 striking machine, weighed 1,000 pounds, and had a diameter of 36 inches and a height of 28 inches. The first fog bells were rung by hand. The lighthouse fog bell system had a weight-and-pulley escapement; the bell machine would run for 3 hours and 15 minutes with one winding, striking a single blow every 15 seconds. Over the years, the weights have rusted in place, but the bell still remains on the lighthouse. Below is the electric foghorn that has replaced the original bell on the Huntington Harbor Lighthouse. (Both, Pam Setchell, Viewpoint Photography.)

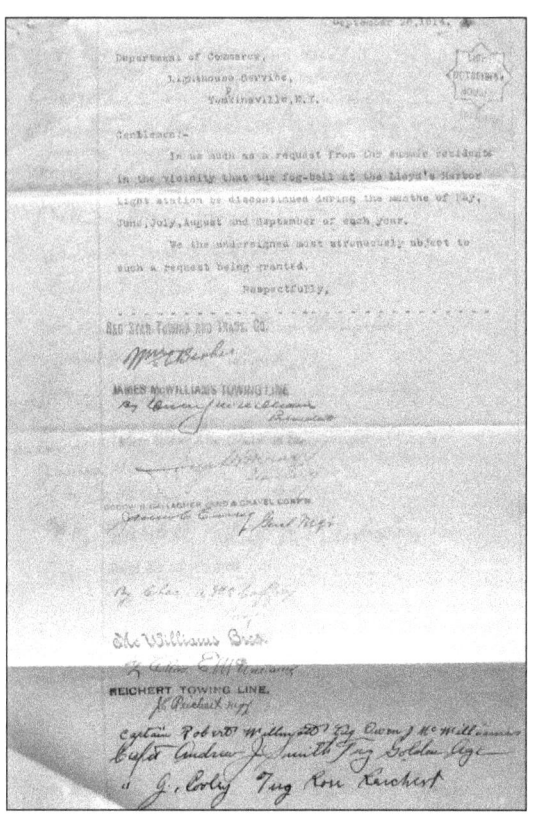

There was a lot of controversy regarding the lighthouse fog bell. Huntingtonians residing by the shore did not see the need for it as much as sloop and freight boat captains. At left is a petition signed by boat captains in 1914 objecting to the discontinuance of the fog bell from May through September every year. Below is a letter of complaint from August Heckscher with great concern about the fog bell constantly ringing when fog occurred in the bay, the harbor, or the sound. The bell kept him and his neighbors awake all night. He stated that there were few if any boats entering the harbor at night because of the tides. Therefore, he believed that the old lighthouse was far better placed and more efficient than the newly erected lighthouse. (Both, National Archives.)

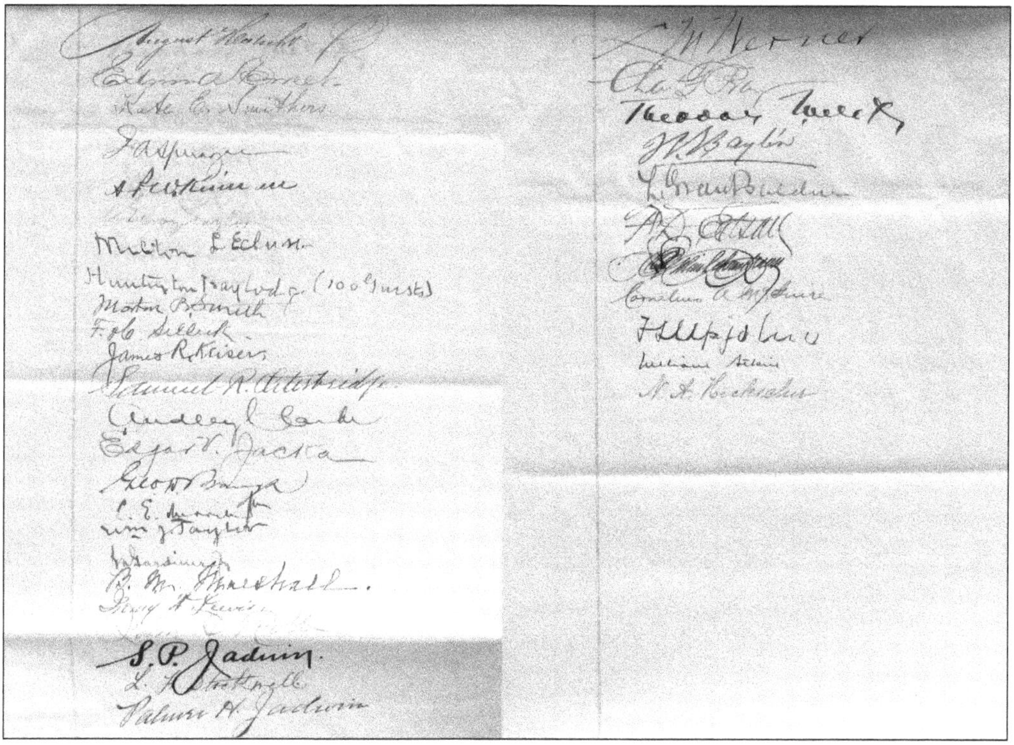

A petition was signed by town residents in 1914 opposing the fog bell during the summer months. Among them was August Heckscher, whose house was in Wincoma, a very exclusive area to the south of the lighthouse. (National Archives.)

JTY/EJC.

626

July 24th, 1914.

Robert McGlone, Keeper,
Lloyd Harbor Light Station,
Huntington, L.I., N.Y.

A complaint has been received at this office that the fog bell at Lloyd Harbor Light greatly annoys the residents of the vicinity, especially those owning summer homes on or near the shore in the vicinity of the Light Station.

It is desired to cause as little annoyance to these people as possible, and you are hereby directed to sound the bell at this station only at such time as the fog is sufficiently thick to make same necessary.

As a guide as to when bell should be sounded, the gas buoy at Northport entrance is to be used, and bell sounded only when the light on this buoy is obscured at night, and the buoy itself during the day time.

YATES.
Inspector.

To settle the complaints of the Huntington summer-home owners about the fog bell, inspector Joseph T. Yates sent a letter to the lighthouse keeper. He directed him to sound the bell only when the fog was sufficiently thick. The gas buoy at the Northport entrance was to be used as a guide, and the bell was to be sounded only when the light on this buoy was obscured at night and the buoy itself was obscured during the daytime. (National Archives.)

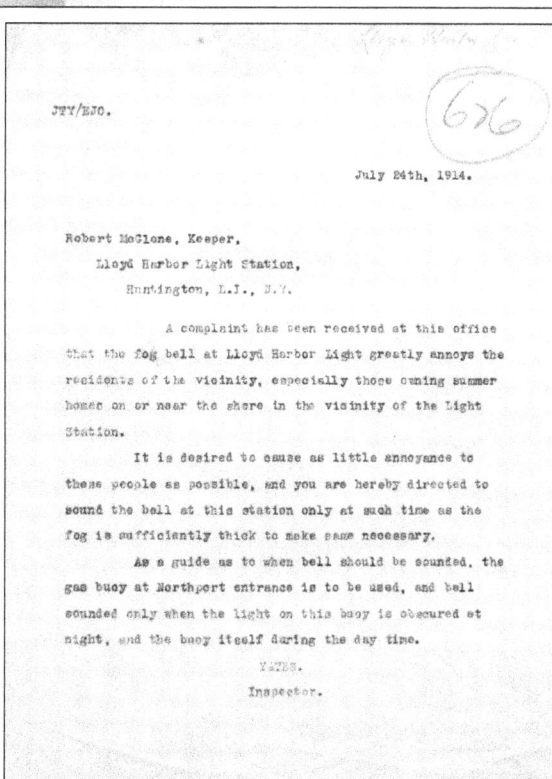

In 1989, the nonprofit group Save Huntington Lighthouse Inc. hired divers to check if the brick chimney was part of the lighthouse's foundation. It was not. (Huntington Lighthouse Archives.)

A letter from August Heckscher on July 27, 1914, conveys the wishes of Huntington shorefront residents who preferred to have the old lighthouse continued and divert the $45,000 appropriated for the new lighthouse to improving the depth of Huntington Harbor. To that amount, Heckscher offered an additional $5,000. He was informed that the appropriation had been made and could not be diverted. The only option would be cancellation of the project. (National Archives.)

A partial list of boats shows those entering Huntington Harbor in 1914 and using the lighthouse as a navigation guide. Most of them were freight steamboats and shellfish sloops. (National Archives.)

A page from the keeper's log in November 1948 lists all the activities that were necessary to prepare the lighthouse prior to its automation by the Coast Guard in 1949. It took the lightkeeper more than five days to pack all the equipment, which was eventually taken to the Eatons Neck Light Station. (National Archives.)

After automation in 1949, and with lack of maintenance of the building, the condition of the lighthouse slowly started to deteriorate. By 1985, the lighthouse was in such disrepair that the Coast Guard was ready to demolish it and erect a steel tower. The lighthouse was saved due to protests from boaters and a group of town residents led by Janis Harrington, a teacher from Greenlawn, who organized Save Huntington Lighthouse Inc. (National Archives.)

Looking to the north from the lantern deck of the lighthouse, one can see Long Island Sound. Twelve miles away in the background is Connecticut. In the far distance to the right is the Eatons Neck Lighthouse, which is operated by the US Coast Guard. To the left is Lloyd Harbor, which has always been rich in clay beds. The Crossman Brick Company, dating to 1760, utilized this clay to make bricks. (Ethan Sands and Pam Setchell, Viewpoint Photography.)

Three

LIGHTKEEPERS

Lloyd Harbor Station Keepers

John S. Wood	June 4, 1857-August 11, 1857
Abiatha Johnson	August 11, 1857 – May 17, 1861
Alanson Pearsall	May 17, 1861 – September 2, 1861
Abiatha Johnson	September 2, 1861 – May 4, 1869
Capt. Lester C. Darling	May 4, 1869 – April 13, 1874
George R. Johnson	April 13, 1874 – November 8, 1884
Neal Ward	November 10, 1884 – September 26, 1885
Robert T. McGlone	September 26, 1885 – June 15, 1912

Huntington Harbor Lighthouse Keepers

Robert T. McGlone	June 16, 1912 – January 31, 1919
Marvin Burnham	March 31, 1919 – September 30, 1926
James Galler	October 1, 1926 – March 16, 1928
Andrew Zuius	March 17, 1928 – March 14, 1929
Emil J. Brunner	March 15, 1929 – June 29, 1930
Joseph Dubois	June 30, 1930 – July 1, 1933
Robert Howard	July 2, 1933 – October 31, 1935
Arthur Bouder	January 1, 1935 – March 31, 1938
Richard J. White	April 1, 1938 – December 31, 1942
Bernard A. Bentley	December 31, 1942 – March 23, 1943
Richard J. White	March 24, 1943 – May 19, 1948
Arnold Leiter, USCG	August 27 – November 22, 1948

Substitute Keepers (Usually signified by change of hand-writing in keepers' log. All serving from one week to one month)

1915 Nov.11 - 24	un-named
February 1, 1919 – March 31, 1919	John Grimes
1930 December	Robert Sammis
1931 December	John Morrisse
1933 Oct. 7 - 12	Kingston H. Ross
1934 and 1935 (summer)	Louis (Louie) Anderson
1937 (various dates)	Tony Ackles
1938 March 13 - 31	Mr. Snitka

January 1945 to April 1945
George L Jilke (cox), John Merry (MO), Stewart H. Carter (BM 1/C), Louis Anderson, David Joseph (CM/ 3C)

May 20, 1948 to November 22, 1948
Sven Eshenbaum, Peter Rossano, Richard Simpson, Frank Souza, Joseph Thomas and Thomas Torrence - all served from 1 or 2 weeks
(Courtesy Steve Eckers)

This is a timeline of all the lightkeepers who served on both the Lloyd Harbor Light Station and the Huntington Harbor Lighthouse. (Steve Eckers.)

On June 4, 1857, John S. Wood was appointed keeper of the Lloyd Harbor Light Station at the annual salary of $350. His vacation was August 11, 1857, at which time he declined to return to the keeper's position. Abiatha Jonhson was then appointed keeper. The date of his vacation was May 17, 1861, at which time he was removed from the position. The same day, Alanson Pearsall was appointed keeper with the same salary until September 2, 1861. Then Abiatha Johnson returned at an increased salary of $520 until May 4, 1869, when he was removed again and L.C. Darling accepted the position. (National Archives.)

> The new light house on Lloyd's Neck Beach, at the entrance of the Harbor, was lighted for the first time on Sunday night last, the 15th inst. Abiatha Johnson, of this village, is keeper.

A local newspaper announced that the Lloyd Harbor Light Station was lighted for the first time on Sunday, November 15, 1857, and Abiatha Jonhson, of the same village, was the keeper. (Huntington Historical Society.)

On April 4, 1861, Commodore Hiram Paulding recommended that Abiatha Johnson, keeper of the Lloyd Harbor Light Station, be retained in his position. There are no records indicating why Johnson was removed in May 1861 for almost four months, but records from the National Archives indicate that he returned in September. (National Archives.)

On March 17, 1869, James Parker, from the Atlantic Mutual Insurance Company of New York, recommended Capt. L.C. Darling for the position as keeper of the Lloyd Harbor Light Station. Darling was appointed on May 4, 1869, replacing Abiatha Johnson. (National Archives.)

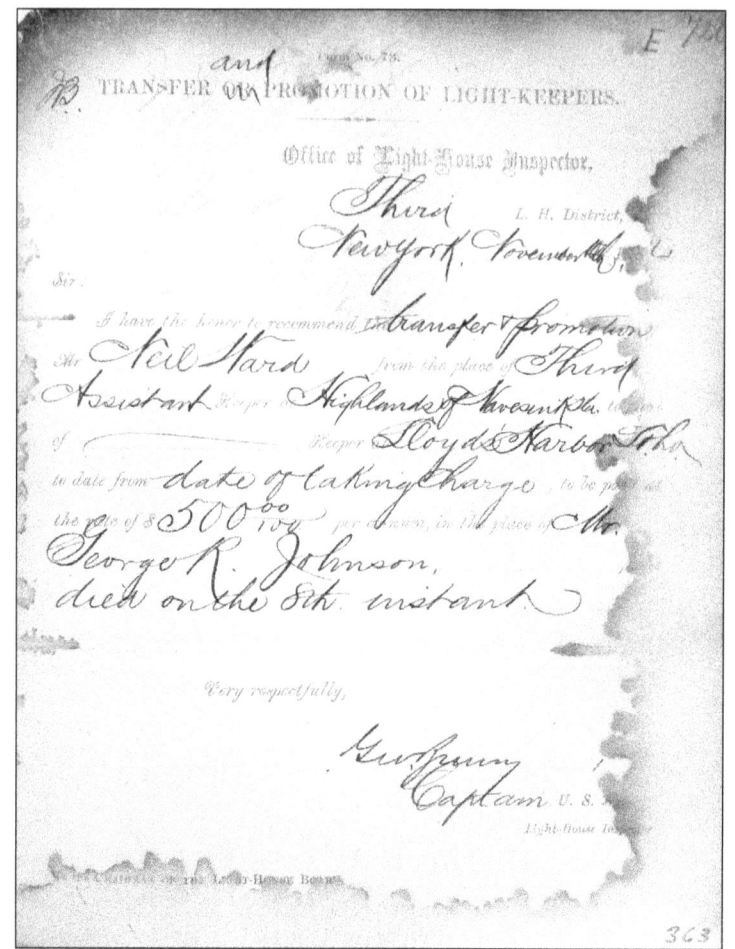

A letter from the office of the lighthouse inspector, Third District, dated November 10, 1884, recommended Neil Ward to be the seventh lightkeeper at Lloyd Harbor following George R. Johnson, who had died two days earlier. His salary was to be $500 per year. Prior to this, Ward was third assistant keeper at Highlands of Navesink Station. (National Archives.)

Pictured are the death records of keeper Robert McGlone and his wife, Margaret Spring McGlone. He died on February 7, 1919, at the age of 62 of a cerebral hemorrhage and chronic lead poisoning. She died at the age of 33 as a result of cardiac failure and hematemesis (traumatic post-operative bleeding) following a hysterectomy. She left five young children, the oldest 14 and the youngest three. (Huntington Town Clerk's Archives.)

This is the gravestone of Robert T. McGlone, who served as keeper of the Lloyd Harbor Light Station from September 26, 1885, to June 15, 1912. He replaced Neil Ward. McGlone was transferred to the Huntington Harbor Lighthouse on June 16, 1912, thus becoming the first keeper of this lighthouse. He retired on January 31, 1919. (Steve Eckers.)

Augusta Harrigan was trained as a caretaker while growing up on the Denton farm, where her parents had moved from Ireland in the 1890s. She first came to the Lloyd Harbor Light Station in 1900 to keep house for Robert McGlone and raise his five children after McGlone's wife died. She remained as the caretaker of the station long after McGlone was transferred to the new lighthouse in 1912 and the children had left. (Huntington Historical Society.)

A June 4, 1928, letter from the Long Island State Park Commission to William Trainer, Huntington town clerk, informed him that a resolution was passed authorizing the issuance of a permit transferring the land of the Lloyd Harbor Light Station to the Town of Huntington. The commission also inquired if the town would continue to pay the caretaker's wage. Anna (Augusta) Harrigan was receiving $50 per month from the commission, but that arrangement was set to expire on July 1, 1928. (National Archives.)

Harrigan sent a letter to Huntington town clerk W.B. Trainer on January 15, 1931, attesting to salary and compensation reimbursement. Originally, the state paid her $50 per month to be the caretaker of the Lloyd Harbor Light Station while the lighthouse lands were under state jurisdiction. In 1928, the station's reservation lands became the responsibility of the Town of Huntington. This outcome was not in Harrigan's favor. (Huntington Town Clerk's Archives.)

> The question of what the town will do with the Lloyd Neck Lighthouse property is
>
> The question is being asked "What is the town going to do with the Lloyd Harbor Lighthouse property?" Miss Harrigan, the who has occupied the building, and acts as a custodian, has resigned, and many applications for the position have been received by the Town Board. Miss has lived at the lighthouse for many years acting as housekeeper for the late Robert McGlone.

On October 1, 1934, the 65-year-old Augusta Harrigan resigned as caretaker of the Lloyd Harbor Light Station. The $25-per-month salary offered to her by the Town of Huntington was not sufficient for her livelihood. As per this note, the Huntington Town Board was reviewing applications, but nobody had been chosen as yet. (Huntington Town Clerk's Archives.)

Michael Fish was the caretaker at the Lloyd Harbor Light Station on or about 1935, after Augusta Harrigan retired. His granddaughter Evelyn M. Reilly remembers spending many happy summer days there. She remembers her grandfather sharpening his spears to go eeling at night. She recalls, "We were never hungry. There were always lots of seafood and clambakes on the beach." (Evelyn Reilly.)

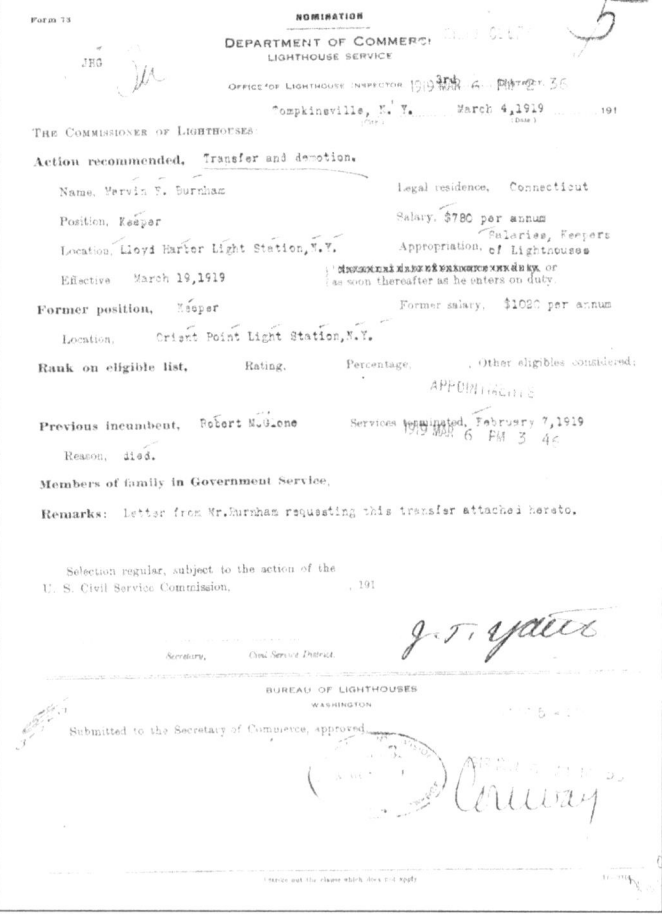

Lightkeeper Marvin Edward Burnham, posing on the landing of the Huntington Harbor Lighthouse, was keeper from March 31, 1919, to September 30, 1926. Prior to this appointment, he was the lightkeeper at Orient Point Light Station. As indicated at left, his transfer to the Huntington Harbor Lighthouse was considered a demotion, as his salary at Orient Point was $1,020 per annum and was cut down to $780 at the Huntington Harbor Lighthouse. He chose this appointment in Huntington because it was more conducive to his family needs. At the time of his resignation, he was receiving a salary of $1,320. He was succeeded by James Galler, who served from October 1, 1926, through March 19, 1928. (Both, Charles Burnham Jr.)

Charles Burnham, son of lightkeeper Marvin Burnham, lived at the Huntington Harbor Lighthouse with his parents. He kept his bicycle on the lighthouse. Every day, he loaded it on the boat, took it on shore, and rode it to school. He attended Huntington High School when it was located on Main Street where the east wing of Huntington Town Hall is today. (Huntington Lighthouse Archives.)

Keeper Burnham recommended that his son Charles Burnham serve as the substitute lightkeeper any time he took a leave of absence or went on vacation. There is evidence of two instances when Marvin had to leave the lighthouse for three to four days, first to tend to his father and later to attend his father's funeral. (Charles Burnham Jr.)

Copy NJL

Holesite

Inspector Tompkinsville

Dear Sir

I see the keeper of the Loyds Harbor Light Station has gone on his vacation and left his son in charge he thinks he is comp in every respect no doubt. the keeper went on Friday and on Saturday the lad was up to Huntington selling hard clams and again was away on Monday. who was looking after the station while he was away. I am a clamer and this may seem like malice but I do think if both father and son is drawing a salary from the government they might be satisfied. the lad says he is on a two months vacation

Sincerely

a clamer

A letter sent by a fisherman informs an inspector that the keeper's son left the lighthouse unattended for two days to sell clams in Huntington while he was in charge of the lighthouse during his father's two-month vacation. Since the letter has no date, it can only be assumed that it refers to young Charles Burnham, who performed the duties of the lightkeeper every time his father, Marvin Burnham, was away. (National Archives.)

Life was monotonous at the Huntington Harbor Lighthouse, which was located in the middle of the water. The keeper and his family entertained themselves with the very little means available to them. Second from left is Elizabeth Lucinda Chapel Burnham, wife of keeper Marvin Burnham. Marvin is second from right. At far right is possibly Augusta Harrigan, caretaker of the Lloyd Harbor Light Station. (Huntington Lighthouse Archives.)

Marvin Burnham is pictured with an inspector on a tender, probably during a visit to the lighthouse. Lighthouse keeper was a civil service position. Inspectors visited lighthouses to check the condition of the structures and the proper operation of the lights. If the light tower and apparatus were not in spic-and-span condition, the keeper received a warning. After three warnings, he could lose his job. (Huntington Lighthouse Archives.)

Andrew Zuius Jr. began his career in the Lighthouse Service as a young man probably in the early 1920s. The first station at which he is mentioned was Sakonnet Point Lighthouse, Little Compton, Rhode Island. He served as the keeper of the Huntington Harbor Lighthouse from March 17, 1928, to March 14, 1929. (Steve Eckers.)

Louis "Louie" Anderson served as a temporary lightkeeper during the summer from 1934 through 1936. He served as a keeper again in 1945. (Huntington Lighthouse Archives.)

Arnold "Arnie" Leiter is pictured here in 1966. He was the last Coast Guardsman in charge of the Huntington Harbor Lighthouse, starting on August 27, 1948. On November 22, 1948, he locked the door to the lighthouse, as a keeper was no longer needed. The lighthouse went on automatic control from Eatons Neck. (Veronika Bleakley.)

Four
Huntington Harbor Lighthouse Restoration, 1985–2010

A Statement of Need Q-976 (a survey) for the Huntington Harbor Lighthouse was ordered by the US Coast Guard in October 1985. The estimated cost for rehabilitating and restoring the lighthouse at that time came to the staggering amount of $650,000. The Coast Guard was not in a position financially to restore the lighthouse. (Huntington Lighthouse Archives.)

Save the Huntington Lighthouse Inc. accepted responsibility for restoring and maintaining the lighthouse in 1985. Both the interior and exterior of the structure were in need of significant repairs. Cracks in the upper-structure masonry work around the lighthouse had allowed water to seep through the concrete walls, resulting in failure of the interior plaster surfaces. Seven arched wooden windows needed to be replaced. The concrete foundation, as shown below, as well as the base and the landing of the lighthouse, had also been eroded and damaged due to high tide, occasional northeasterly storms, and boat traffic in Huntington Bay. (Both, Huntington Lighthouse Archives.)

During the restoration of 1985, the seriously damaged cabinets pictured above were found in the living quarters. The furniture, which was original to the lighthouse, has been restored and is used today for storage. The built-in cabinets seen below were located in the storage area of the basement and were original to the structure as well. They have also been salvaged and remain in the basement. (Both, Huntington Lighthouse Archives.)

Save the Huntington Lighthouse Inc. received funding from the New York State Parks Office of Historic Preservation for the purpose of restoring the lighthouse. With this funding and many hours of volunteer work, repairs to the concrete structure were initiated in 1985 and continued for many years. At left, the ladder leading to the landing was replaced in 1990 by a floating dock and ramp, which allowed visitors to access the lighthouse. Prior to that, entrance to the lighthouse was achieved by climbing the ladder attached to the landing on the west side of the lighthouse. (Above, Valerie Whyte; left, Huntington Lighthouse Archives.)

Above, volunteers deliver the new access ramp to the lighthouse via boat. At right, volunteers are cleaning and scraping the lighthouse's concrete foundation where the landing platform and the entrance ramp were to be placed. (Both, Huntington Lighthouse Archives.)

As seen in both of these images, the extensive damage to the lighthouse involved exterior cracks throughout the whole structure. Water had seeped through both the cupola and the cracks and caused major damage to the interior. Also noticeable were large gouged-out areas on the stairs, holes in the foundation, and the total deterioration of the railing. (Both, Huntington Lighthouse Archives.)

Steve and Jonathan Weingarten and foreman Bryan McLeod from the General Restoration Company in the Bronx were awarded the restoration bid. Their first priority was to examine the cracks in the base of the lighthouse prior to obtaining concrete samples for analysis. Under the terms of the contract, the loose concrete from the base had to be removed and replaced. The cracks, fissures, and cavities also had to be repaired. As shown below, another issue was the roof, which had collapsed due to the lack of maintenance. More funding was received in 1996 and was allocated toward repairing the roof. (Both, Huntington Lighthouse Archives.)

There are 11 sections of railings, each 48 inches long, amounting to approximately 44 linear feet of rails on all three levels of the lighthouse. When Save the Huntington Lighthouse Inc. assumed responsibility for the lighthouse, half of the railings were missing. Those sections were installed during the early restoration efforts and were made to stand along with the remaining sections. The railings that had been less compromised were repaired. All the rails were scraped, primed, and painted. Below, volunteer Henry Bungart secures the railings on the perimeter of the first floor. (Both, Huntington Lighthouse Archives.)

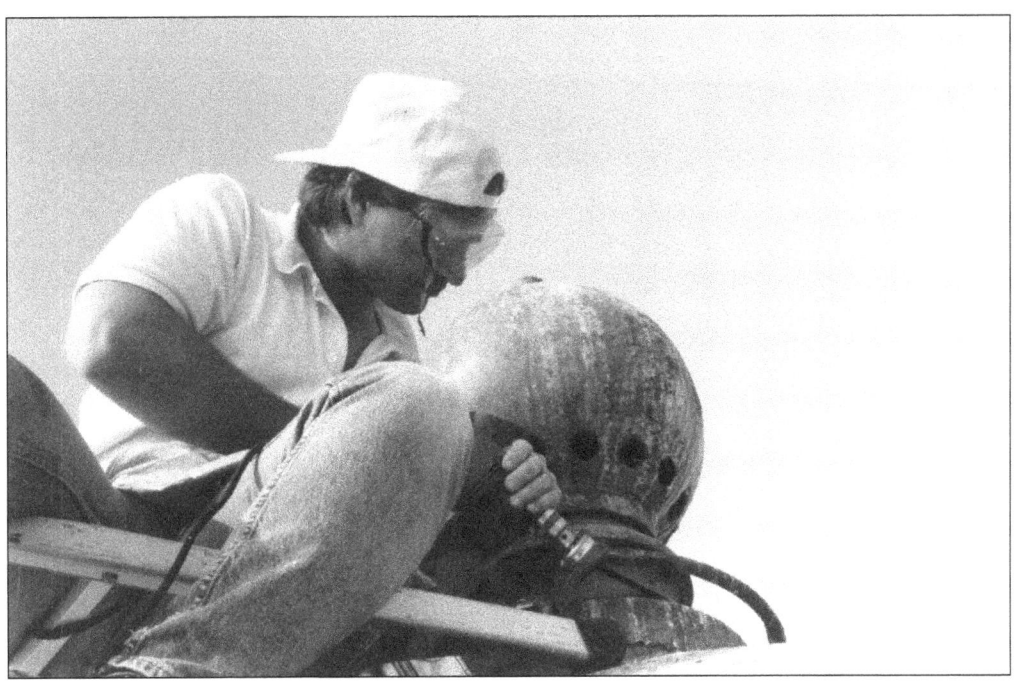

These two pictures are of the lighthouse cupola roof. Replacing it had not been feasible or cost-effective, because the original panels that were made in 1912 were no longer available 80 years later. The restoration effort in 1990 included reconstructing the rod details of the cupola and welding the existing holes. (Both, Huntington Lighthouse Archives.)

The dumbwaiter in the living quarters was used by the lightkeeper to bring up coal for the potbelly stove to heat the lighthouse and oil or kerosene for the lantern from the basement. In 2004, it was rebuilt, and is still in working order. (Huntington Lighthouse Archives.)

The narrow and winding spiral staircase, built around a large hollow column, allows access from the basement up to the watch deck. The staircase had deteriorated and was unsafe; the environmental conditions of salt, water, and air resulted in the metal steps becoming eroded. (Huntington Lighthouse Archives.)

These two images of the interior show the first floor of the lighthouse, the living quarters, prior to the restoration in 2003. There was no running water or electricity in the structure, making the restoration more challenging. In the interior living space, the bedroom was separated from the living room by a closet. During renovation, the upper part of the closet was removed. A counter was installed in its place that today allows for multiple uses, such as buffet food service. (Both, Huntington Lighthouse Archives.)

These images show the woodwork labor that went into restoring the lighthouse. All interior woodwork, such as wainscoting, base and crown moldings, and hardwood floors were fabricated according to the original plans. The wood that was used to repair the floor and the roof rafters was cut and refined at the Harned Sawmill, a local company. Then it was brought to the lighthouse and stored on the first floor until needed. (Both, Huntington Lighthouse Archives.)

The interior walls of the lighthouse had no insulation. During restoration, new wire lath and plaster finish over terra-cotta furring tiles were installed to restore the walls and ceilings. The interior walls were painted according to the requirements of the New York State Standards for Historic Preservation. The original color was seafoam green, which has been maintained to this day. (Huntington Lighthouse Archives.)

Volunteers work on the lighthouse ceiling. Labor was free and people were willing to work to help keep the lighthouse standing. (Huntington Lighthouse Archives.)

Tons of concrete were used to plaster the interior walls. Here, professional mason Denato Gustierferro applies plaster to the walls of the living quarters. Gustierferro, like so many other dedicated individuals, volunteered his services. (Both, Huntington Lighthouse Archives.)

From 1988 through 1998, major accomplishments were achieved in the restoration of the lighthouse, one of which was replacing and restoring the seven arched wooden windows. The original windows were made of wavy glass, which was found in older window panels, doors, and furniture built prior to the 19th century. Robin Lindstadt, a professional woodworker, assisted with the repair, installation, and upkeep of the windows. At right are the restored windows. They are accurate reproductions of the originals. (Both, Huntington Lighthouse Archives.)

In 1949, the US Coast Guard automated the lighthouse. Unfortunately, in 2002, the cable that brought power to the lighthouse was damaged. Shortly after that, the Coast Guard installed solar panels that charge the batteries, which in turn supply power to the lamp and the foghorn. (Both, Huntington Lighthouse Archives.)

Five

Huntington Harbor Lighthouse Foundation Rehabilitation, 2011

In 2013, Newport Engineering was hired to perform a topographic survey of the lighthouse foundation and prepare design plans. The survey was used to get a scope of the work needed for the restoration and rehabilitation of the foundation and to arrive at alternatives. The first phase to rehabilitate the foundation commenced in June 2016. A barge and a grapple were used to remove the rock and expose a large area of the corner down to the mud line and across the back wall so that it could be closely examined. (Pam Setchell, Viewpoint Photography.)

NYS Environmental Protection Fund

Huntington Lighthouse Foundation & Stabilization

Huntington Lighthouse Preservation Society.Inc

Andrew M. Cuomo Governor
Rose Harvy, Commissioner

· Frank P. Petrone Huntington Town Supervisor

In June 2011, the Huntington Lighthouse Preservation Society Inc. received grant funding of $250,000 from the New York State Parks Office of Historic Preservation to repair and rehabilitate the lighthouse's foundation. The society raised an additional $600,000 through fundraisers, donations, tours, and other events. (Antonia S. Mattheou.)

The deterioration of the lighthouse's foundation was extensive. Spalled sections of concrete were noted in multiple locations exposing the original three-quarter-inch steel reinforcement. The exterior concrete covering, which typically is a minimum of three inches, had deteriorated to the point of exposing the rebar. (Pam Setchell, Viewpoint Photography.)

Exploratory excavation was done during the Christmas holiday of 2013 to determine the extent of the damage to the foundation. The concern was to find out whether or not the deterioration had spread across the foundation or if it was limited to just the corners. (Pam Setchell, Viewpoint Photography.)

During the planning period, the engineer used the existing US Coast Guard geodetic tidal benchmarks embedded in the lighthouse. These benchmarks provided elevations and established a baseline table of vertical control of the four sides of the building. This benchmark is on the west corner of the lighthouse structure and can be seen by visitors on the way to the staircase that leads to the living space. (Pam Setchell, Viewpoint Photography.)

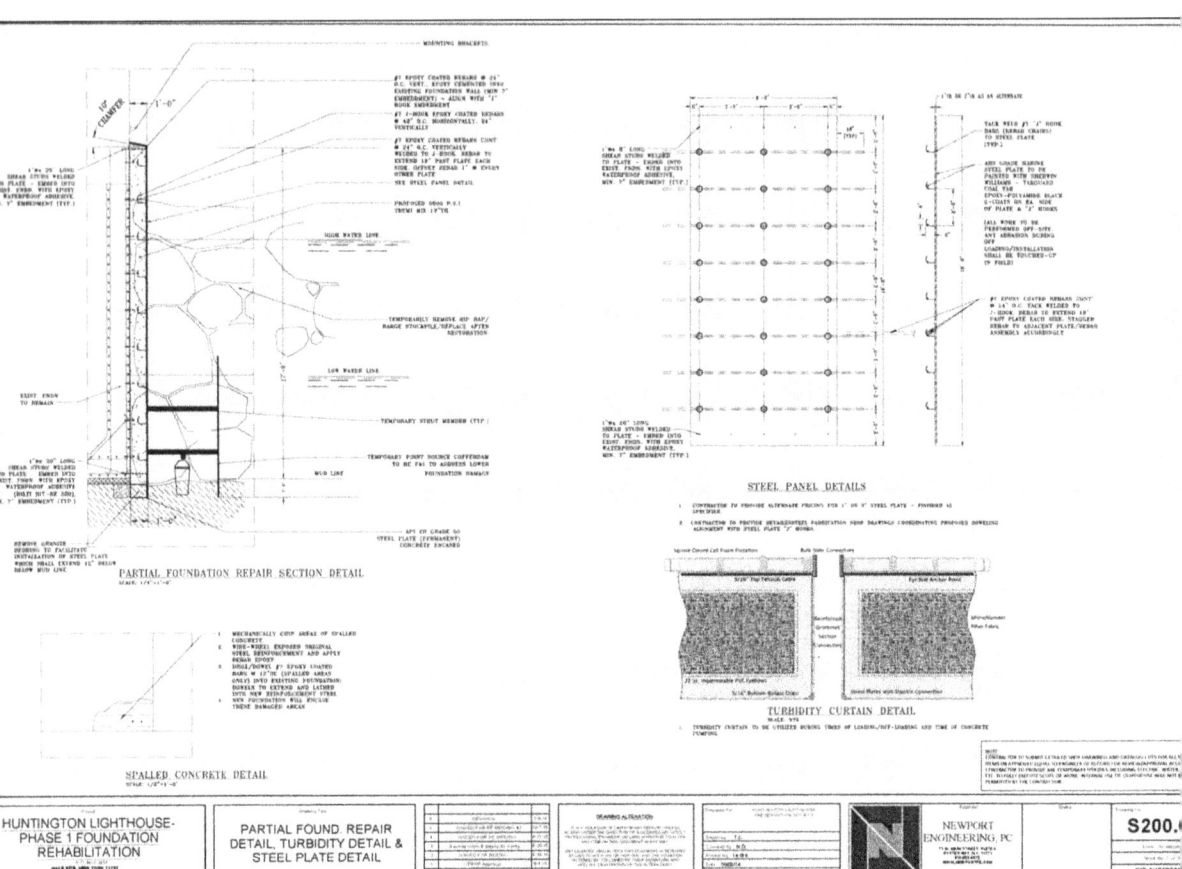

The original plan called for the isolation and repairs of three sides of the foundation. It indicated a permanent installation of steel sheeting, serving as a cofferdam, and concrete infill between the sheeting and the existing square of the lighthouse. Riprap would then be reinstalled accordingly. (Newport Engineering.)

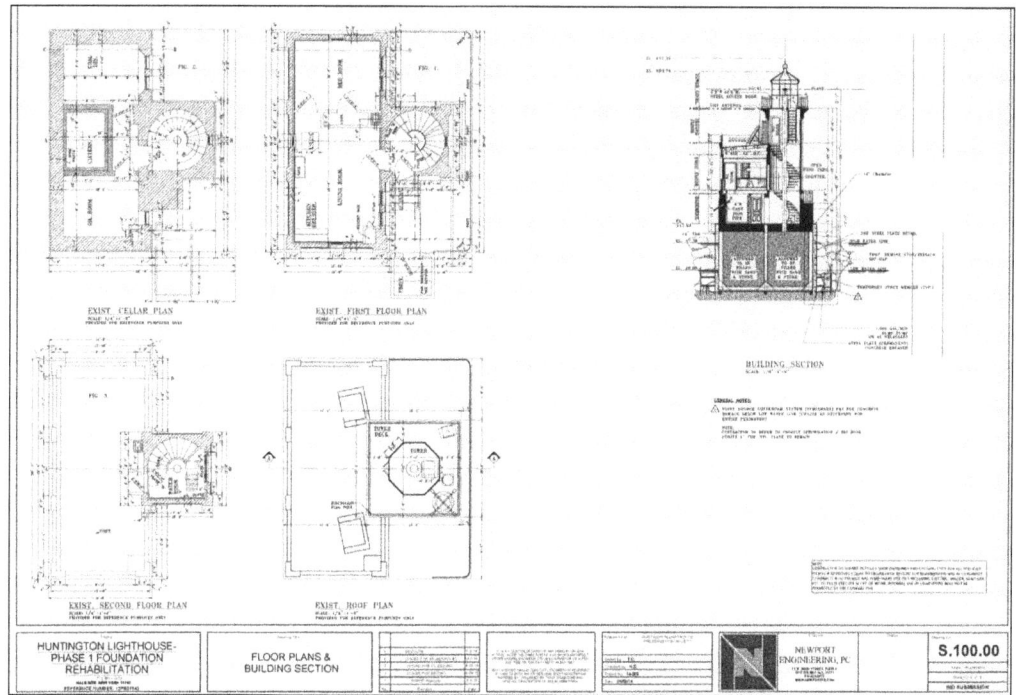

As shown here, two remedial alternatives were presented as approaches for the rehabilitation of the foundation. Alternative No. 1 would utilize steel sheeting to serve as a cofferdam, vibrate in place, and isolate the three foundation sides, providing full protection to the entire wall face. Alternative No. 2 called for bolting steel plates to the original foundation to protect it during tide swings. Although this was an easier application, it did not address the foundation area below the low-tide mark should further damage be uncovered during construction. The first option was chosen. (Above, Newport Engineering; below, Ed Carr.)

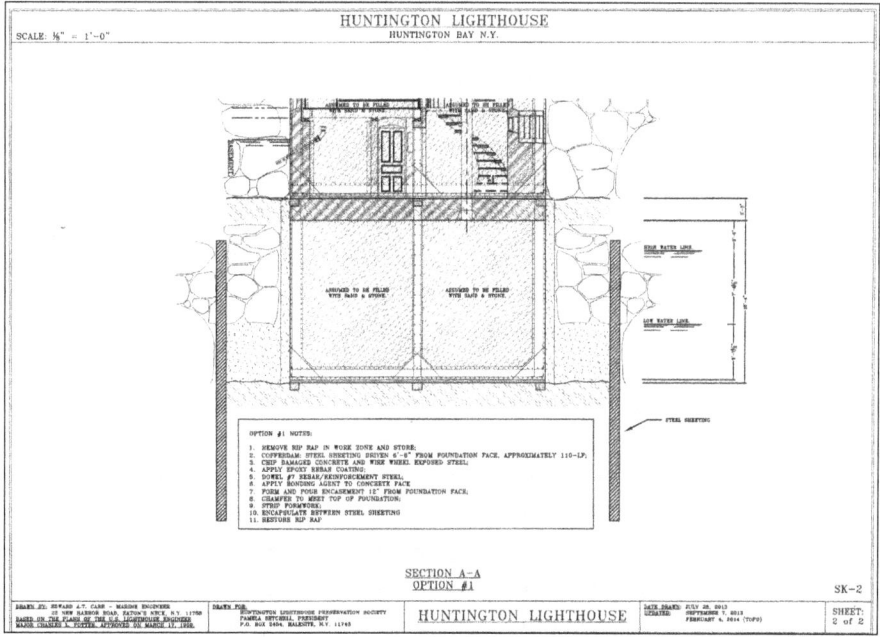

Scobbo Foundation Systems was hired in 2013 to explore the extent of the damage to the underwater foundation. This firm is known for its expertise in underwater foundation repair and was the bidder chosen to rehabilitate and restore the foundation several years later. The picture below shows Scobbo Foundation's dedicated workers reviewing their completed project. Despite looking at their backs, surely they were all smiles and proud of work well done. (Both, Doug Martines.)

A Volvo EC 240 excavator with long reach (over 40 feet) and grapple was used to remove the riprap from around the lighthouse. The riprap was first used when the lighthouse was constructed in 1912 to protect the structure's concrete face against scour and to serve as an impact energy dissipater. Scour, the rubbing away of concrete, occurs due to years of tidal action, water elevation changes, and ice erosion. (Both, Pam Setchell, Viewpoint Photography.)

Prior to the rehabilitation of the foundation, prep work needed to be done. That included removing the delaminated concrete, scarifying the surface, wire-wheeling the original three-quarter-inch-square steel reinforcement, and treating the raw steel with spray epoxy. Upon completion of this process, steel sheeting was installed and a concrete encasement approximately 12 to 18 inches thick was poured, as seen below. (Both, Pam Setchell, Viewpoint Photography.)

Shown in these two pictures is the corrugated steel sheeting that was brought to the lighthouse site by barge. Each piece was carefully hoisted into position, guided by the skilled workmen, and placed around the foundation. (Both, Pam Setchell, Viewpoint Photography.)

This image shows how the plates interlocked. They measured three quarters of an inch thick. The installation involved carefully setting the sheeting into place around the lighthouse foundation to provide toe beneath the existing seabed. The steel sheeting was anchored within the internal steel reinforcement cage and the new assembly doweled to the existing foundation for full encapsulation. (Newport Engineering.)

The prep work and repairs to the original foundation were completed shortly before Christmas 2017. To isolate the three foundation sides in order to provide full access to the entire wall, steel sheeting was utilized as a temporary cofferdam to control tidal water and to serve as the permanent exterior steel face, with in situ concrete poured between the original foundation and the sheeting. (Deanna Glassmann.)

Cement was poured into bags on a barge at the Huntington Yacht Club and then quickly transported to the lighthouse, with a crew standing by ready to hoist each bag over to the lighthouse to be poured between the original foundation and the installed steel sheeting, as seen below. It was imperative that this be executed swiftly before the cement hardened in the bags. (Both, Pam Setchell, Viewpoint Photography.)

The steel sheeting is 20 feet deep and completely surrounds the lighthouse foundation. Between the face of the foundation and the steel sheeting, the concrete measures 12 to 18 inches thick. To protect the structure further from tidal action, the riprap that existed before the rehabilitation was placed back around the lighthouse. (Doug Martines.)

As construction progressed toward the south side of the lighthouse, an existing concrete slab (landing pad) resting on top of the riprap was discovered. The design of the south side of the landing was changed several times since the original construction of the lighthouse in 1912. In the mid-1930s, the first dock foundation was doweled into the building. In the 1990s, a steel pier was added by the Coast Guard, and an additional concrete slab was poured over the old concrete landing. (Pam Setchell, Viewpoint Photography.)

While excavating the southernmost section of the lighthouse foundation, part of the already compromised landing platform collapsed. The entire concrete platform, consisting of two platforms (one over the other), had to be removed and broken up. This dramatic event forced a change to the original scope of work for the fourth side, incurring a tremendous change in the cost of the project. Emergency fundraising began immediately. (Pam Setchell, Viewpoint Photography.)

Throughout years of freezes, thaws, and tidal action, the lighthouse experienced shifting of the protective riprap, which caused the landing platform to deteriorate. (Pam Setchell, Viewpoint Photography, and Newport Engineering.)

In June 2017, the Robert D.L. Gardiner Foundation awarded the society $145,000 to rehabilitate and repair the southeast side of the lighthouse. The money allowed the contractor to excavate the fourth side and continue with the steel sheeting and associated steel reinforcement to the existing concrete foundation along this wall. The additional work was approximately 28 linear feet of further debris removal, installation of steel sheeting, and infilling with 5,000-pound-per-square-inch concrete. (Antonia S. Mattheou.)

This is what the south side of the foundation looked like prior to rehabilitation. The west side had just been completed, with the steel sheeting in place and the concrete poured. However, a portion of the rebar remained exposed to be used for the final tie-in to the landing platform after the repair of the south side. This never happened. Instead, the landing platform was replaced. (Antonia S. Mattheou.)

In the fall of 2017, the removal of the riprap covering the fourth side of the lighthouse began. To reach the lighthouse, one has to get from a boat to a floating dock, walk up a steel pier to a landing platform, climb up a few steel steps, and then climb the steps to the lighthouse entrance. Below, a crane removes the existing steel pier. This was necessary in order to demolish what remained of the landing platform, which was attached to the pier. (Both, Pam Setchell, Viewpoint Photography.)

These two photographs show parts of the davit (a cranelike device) found while removing the riprap from the southeast side of the lighthouse. Between 1935 and 1945, the lightkeeper used a davit to pull his boat onto the landing, which had a different design than the one used today. (Both, Antonia S. Mattheou.)

An ornate piece of concrete, possibly part of the old landing platform dating to 1935, was unearthed while excavating the southeast corner. The entrance and landing platform were located at this side in the 1930s. That part of the landing platform was replaced by steel during the recent rehabilitation of the foundation. (Antonia S. Mattheou.)

From the time the rehabilitation of the south side started in the fall of 2017 until June 2018, when the new landing platform was installed, there was no access to the lighthouse. The US Coast Guard, which maintains the lighthouse, had to utilize a ladder to climb to the platform in order to access it. The ladder leading from the water to the steel pier, the landing platform, and the steps leading to the lighthouse entrance had to be removed, as shown here. (Pam Setchell, Viewpoint Photography.)

Completion of the last pour of concrete on the landing platform marked the total rehabilitation of the underwater foundation for the first time since 1912. A total of 30 feet of steel sheeting, each measuring 20 feet in length, was installed on this side. A new epoxy-coated rebar cage and angle iron tie braces match the other three sides. By December 2017, the rehabilitation of the south side of the foundation was almost completed, as pictured below. This allowed for the new encasement of steel sheeting and concrete to surround all four sides of the lighthouse foundation. (Both, Pam Setchell, Viewpoint Photography.)

In January 2018, the first of the helical piles, which serve as the base for the new landing platform, was drilled in. However, bad weather and horridly frigid temperatures resulted in all the barges being demobilized and construction ceasing until March. It is important to remember that this lighthouse is surrounded by water. Although the materials had arrived to continue building the landing platform, construction always remained dependent on the weather. Eventually, as seen below, a total of eight helical piles were drilled in preparation for the construction of the new landing platform. (Both, Pam Setchell, Viewpoint Photography.)

By May 2018, all repairs were made to the south side of the foundation. That included the installation of the steel sheeting to complete a 360-degree encasement of the foundation, the filling of the cofferdam with cement, and the installation of the helical piles as a support base for the new landing platform. As shown at left, once the rehabilitation of the foundation was completed, riprap was placed around it, including under and around the new landing platform. (Both, Pam Setchell, Viewpoint Photography.)

The original plan called for the installation of a concrete platform 8 feet by 20 feet by 1½ feet thick. Galvanized helical piles and associated hardware were utilized. Round helical piles measuring 7 inches in diameter were installed, and greenheart timber materials created the framing and associated deck. As shown below, the original steel pier was reinstalled and attached to the base of the new landing platform. (Both, Pam Setchell, Viewpoint Photography.)

New aluminum railings were fabricated and installed. The new steel landing platform measures 27 feet in length and 13 feet in width. The steel pier leading to the landing platform is 29 feet long. That brings the walkway to the lighthouse to a total of 56 feet. (Antonia S. Mattheou.)

Once the new landing platform was installed, the existing stairs leading to the lighthouse entrance were cut down and made to fit the new platform. Additionally, the riprap was rearranged to further protect the platform. (Pam Setchell, Viewpoint Photography.)

On Thursday afternoon, June 21, 2018, the barge and crew of Scobbo Foundation Systems left the lighthouse. Their job was finally done, two years almost to the day. (Valerie Whyte.)

At the ribbon-cutting ceremony on July 11, 2018, guests admired the newly rehabilitated foundation of the lighthouse. Among the guests were Kathryn Curran, executive director of the Gardiner Foundation, Tracy Christian of the New York State Parks Office of Historic Preservation, members of the New York State Assembly, Suffolk County legislators, and Huntington town officials. (Douglas Martines.)

During the ribbon-cutting ceremony, members of the Huntington Lighthouse Preservation Society, major donors, and honored guests enjoyed a perfect day. (Douglas Martines.)

On the left in this aerial image is the site where the Lloyd Harbor Light Station once stood. That station was destroyed by fire in 1947. To the right is the Huntington Harbor Lighthouse, which is still an active aid to navigation. (Douglas Martines.)

Six
THE ALLURE OF HUNTINGTON HARBOR

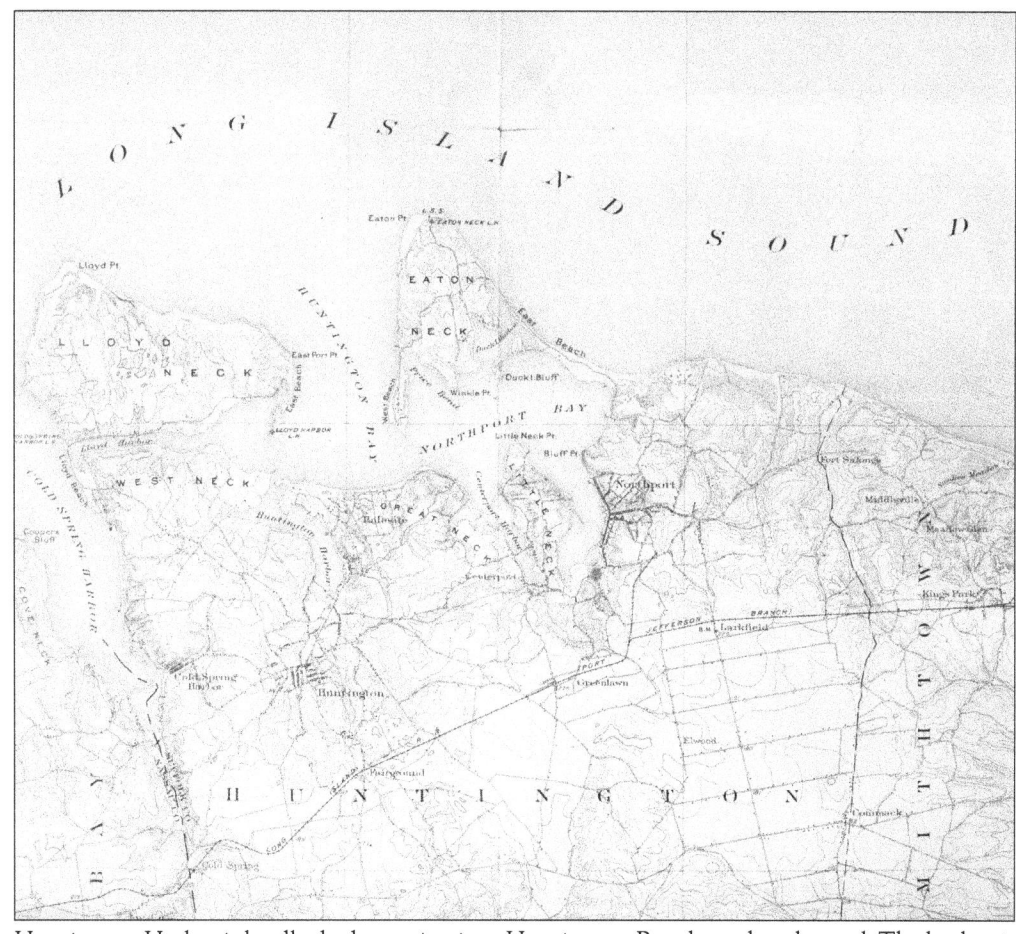

Huntington Harbor is landlocked, opening into Huntington Bay through a channel. The harbor is one of the prettiest views of water found upon the borders of Long Island. The original occupants and businesses of the area that existed 100 years ago are gone, and most of the homes they occupied have also disappeared. Still, Huntington Harbor remains with the everlasting hills surrounding it. (Huntington Town Clerk's Archives.)

All sections of the town's waterfront had problems. In 1933, the Huntington Harbors Improvement Committee was organized to protect and develop all town harbors. On November 3, 1948, the request to improve Huntington Harbor and Bay, signed by town supervisor Walter Fasbender, was approved by the secretary of the Army. It authorized dredging to a depth of 30 feet and using whatever dredged material that could not be sold to backfill the dredged areas. On January 25, 1949, it was agreed to extend the area to be dredged to open the entrance to Huntington Harbor, and the contract was extended to November 1955. (Huntington Town Clerk's Archives.)

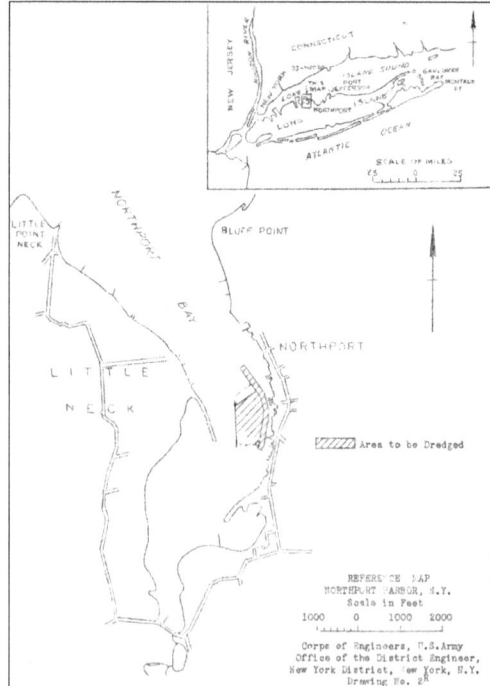

On April 18, 1956, the town paid the US government $15,000, which represented the town's share of the cost of the projected dredging in Northport. It was estimated that a total of 43,200 cubic yards of material would be dredged. The minimum hourly wage paid to dredge scow men and helpers was $1.88. Clamshell dredge operators received $2.87, the highest wage paid. (Huntington Town Clerk's Archives.)

The town trustees hired the United States Dredging Corporation, a subsidiary of Gallagher Brothers of New York, to dredge the harbors. The company had completed a similar project in Oyster Bay and planned to move its immense dredge *Magic City*, which consisted of 55 tugs, to the shores of Connecticut. The original contract was renewed several times due to the extension of the areas to be dredged and other unforeseen circumstances, such as described in the March 19, 1952, letter of Mr. Liefheicht, foreman of the dredge, that informed Dr. Eugene McCauliff of Shore Road that "the operator of the hoist, necessary to the placing of sand on his beach, had suffered a nervous breakdown and would not be at work for a month." (Huntington Town Clerk's Archives.)

With the completion of the dredge, the treacherous, rock-lined, shallow gut or entrance to Huntington Harbor was widened some 300 feet. The section dredged was about 2.5 miles long. Records show that from 1951 to 1952, approximately 512,816 cubic yards of gravel were removed at 9¢ per cubic yard for gravel content less than 40 percent and 10¢ to 11¢ for gravel content 50 percent and over. From December 1955 through November 1956, about 244,439 cubic yards of gravel were removed from Cold Spring and Northport Harbors, and 29,404 cubic yards were removed in April 1957. Profits were used to improve town docks and beaches. This drastic dredging program was completed in 1961 and is considered the most important project undertaken by the Town of Huntington for the improvement of its harbors. Below is an image of *Magic City*. (Both, Huntington Town Clerk's Archives.)

The Cold Spring Harbor Lighthouse was built in 1889 and activated on January 31, 1890. Its square wooden tower, in the shape of a pyramid, rested on a concrete-filled iron caisson. With a focal plane of 40½ feet above mean high water, the beacon was a fourth-order Fresnel lens and had a fixed red light. This was changed to fixed white with a red sector in 1892. During poor visibility, a fog bell struck automatically every 30 seconds. The keeper's boat, housed at the light, was suspended from davits. (US Coast Guard.)

From 1890 through 1942, nineteen keepers served this lighthouse. William S. Keene, the light's first keeper, served for a month before resigning. Returning to the lighthouse on August 3, 1908, keeper Chester Rowland slipped and fell into the water while ascending the station's ladder and drowned. It was reported in the *Suffolk County News* on October 20, 1911, that "John Als. colored, a former assistant keeper at Long Beach Lighthouse, has been appointed keeper at the Cold Spring Harbor Lighthouse." Arthur Jensen served from August 1908 to February 1909. Pres. Theodore Roosevelt and his children visited him regularly. (Pamela Griffin Hansen.)

In 1948, the light was automated, and the Eatons Neck Coast Guard Station accepted responsibility. In 1965, an automated navigation aid was constructed and erected on the original caisson. Lady Glen, a resident of Centre Island, bought the wooden tower for a dollar and planned to place it on her property. She had fond memories of the musical talent of one of the keepers, who played the piano. When the wind blew, she could hear the music from across the water. (Sheriden Schwertl and Thomas Hoffman.)

The Cold Spring Harbor Lighthouse is the only lighthouse on Long Island moved from its original site. Transferring the wooden tower to Lady Glen's property was a challenge. The barge carrying the tower became stuck on a sandbar for a year. Finally, high tide allowed the barge to float off, and the tower was placed on Glen's property overlooking the waters it formerly guarded. (US Coast Guard.)

George Shaw built a house in 1890 overlooking Huntington Bay, and named it the Oaks. John Cartledge purchased the house and enlarged it in 1904, as seen below. The Naval Aviation School, established in 1916, was located here. (Both, Huntington Historical Society.)

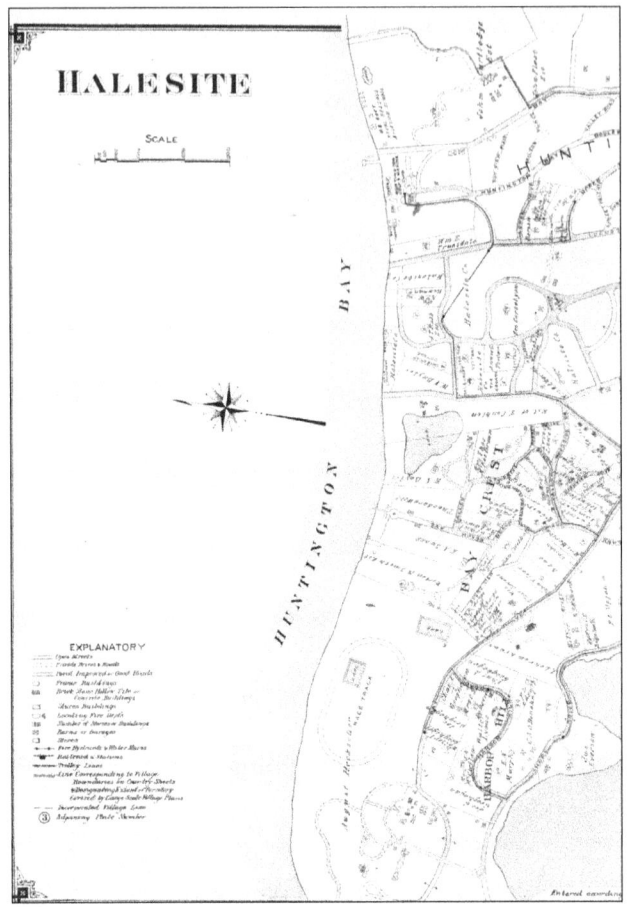

In 1916, the Naval Aviation School was established in Huntington Beach adjacent to the Head of the Bay Club. Frederick Trubee Davison, a Yale University student from Long Island, along with nine of his friends from Yale, created the Yale Unit as part of the school. Attendees completed basic training on single-engine hydroplanes. (Greenlawn Centerport Historical Association.)

The planes flown by Naval Aviation School students were housed in the barn on the Cartledge estate, the Oaks. The Cartledge family's dock was used to pull the planes to and from the beach. The Yale Unit was activated for service in the European theater during the summer of 1917. (Greenlawn Centerport Historical Association.)

A plaque on a rock at the entrance of the Bay Hills pavilion, former site of the Oaks, bears witness to the site of the Yale Unit, which "became legend among all regular and reserve Navy pilots." On July 1, 1966, Frederick Trubee Davison, founder of the unit, was honored by the Navy for his work in naval aviation. (Nancy Y. Moran.)

In early January 1963, the families of the crew of the tugboat *Gwendoline Steers*, who were lost during a fierce 1962 storm, hired the fishing trawler *Tora* to search for the boat and her crew. *Tora* sank while attempting to break out of ice-covered Huntington Harbor. The crew successfully abandoned ship with no loss of life. Raising *Tora* nearly cost a volunteer diver his life when he got lost under the ice. He was spotted 100 feet from shore after wiggling a finger through a small hole in the ice and was rescued. (Oliver Bodine, photograph by Stan Thompson.)

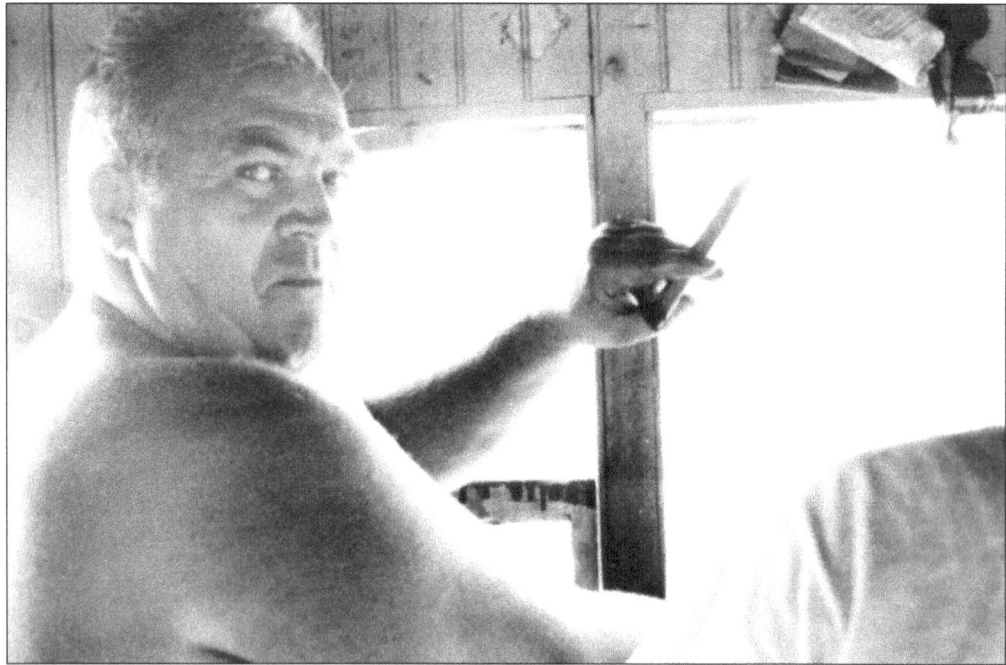

Edwin Townsend, skipper and owner of *Tora*, was an adventurer, entrepreneur, pioneering scuba diver, and cavalier character. He was determined to plow through the ice-encrusted Huntington Harbor to search for *Gwendoline Steers* and her crew. *Tora's* double life as a working dive boat and a party boat was authentic, as evidenced by cases of Rhinegold beer on the aft deck next to the upright piano. After *Tora* sank, parts of the piano were seen floating in the harbor for days. (Oliver Bodine, photograph by Stan Thompson.)

Huntington native and professional diver Stan Thompson crewed on *Tora* in the search mission. When *Tora's* hull was breached, he dashed below to discover the ship taking on large amounts of water. As Ed Townsend tried to maneuver and beach the boat, Thompson yelled up to the wheelhouse, "Ed, we're not going to make it." Despite the crew's frantic efforts, *Tora* sank mere feet from the Huntington Yacht Club. (Oliver Bodine, photograph by Stan Thompson.)

Frank "Doggie" Ellis was employed by the Knutson Boatyard from 1950 to 1980. He started working for his grandfather Thomas Knutson Sr. and stayed working for the family for three generations. Local folklore has it that Doggie was an attorney disbarred during Prohibition. His best friends were two Chesapeake Bay retrievers that were always seen riding with him in one of the Knutson boats in the harbor. On cue, the dogs would jump overboard and retrieve beer cans from the harbor bottom. This story has been attested to by locals in the Huntington Harbor area. (Torkel A. Knutson.)

In 1868, Walter E. Abrams established a boatyard in Huntington Harbor and operated it successfully until his death in 1938. He built wooden boats that the wealthy residents of the town raced in Huntington Harbor. In 1932, Thomas Knutson became a partner, and the name was changed to Abrams & Thomas Knutson Boatyard. (Torkel A. Knutson and Judy Knutson Calabrese.)

Thomas Knutson made improvements to the business by introducing new equipment. When Abrams died, his widow sold the corporation to Knutson. The Thomas Knutson Shipbuilding Corporation is still located in Halesite on Long Island and is known for building pleasure craft of all sizes, both power and sail. Every season, yachtsmen from various harbors on the Eastern Seaboard have their yachts customized here. (Torkel A. Knutson and Judy Knutson Calabrese.)

Above, subchasers are on the assembly line in the Knutson Boatyard. With World War II coming, Thomas Arthur Knutson secured government contracts and commenced building subchasers, landing barges, and oceangoing tugboats. The boatyard received the Certificate of Achievement in recognition of exceptional accomplishments on behalf of the US Navy. Another son, John, managed the shipyard. Below, a landing barge is being tested in front of the Huntington Yacht Club. (Both, Torkel A. Knutson and Judy Knutson Calabrese.)

Above, Thomas Arthur Knutson, son of Thomas Knutson, gets into a 1942 Buick marked "US Navy." The car is still owned by the Knutson family. Below, fuel tanks are ready to be put onto landing barges. Tanks had to be swelled up before being placed in water; otherwise, they would crack. (Both, Torkel A. Knutson and Judy Knutson Calabrese.)

11:—CENTERPORT YACHT CLUB AND POST OFFICE, CENTERPORT, L. I., N. Y.

At the turn of the 20th century, a group of residents interested in sailing established the first yacht club in Centerport. Their clubhouse was located on the piles off the north side of the Mill Dam. This club functioned as a mecca for the local boating aficionados until its demise in the 1930s. (Greenlawn-Centerport Historical Association.)

A new Centerport Yacht Club was formed in 1947, utilizing the Morse mansion as its clubhouse. Below are members of the Morse family enjoying a summer day on the lawn in front of the mansion before the house was sold to the Centerport Yacht Club. The Morse mansion has been expanded and is still used as the clubhouse. The club features an in-ground pool. A young people's swim team competes with other yacht clubs in the area. There is also a sailing school program in the summer as well as fine dining for members. (Both, Greenlawn-Centerport Historical Association.)

In 1876, William and Sarah Clark bought 120 acres in Huntington Bay that stretched roughly to the corner of what is now Vineyard and Cove Roads. The Clarks built a picturesque, privately owned, 44-room Victorian hotel they named Clark House. The Clark House was later sold and operated under the names of Locust Lodge and Huntington Bay Lodge. (Pamela Griffin Hansen.)

Two images of the Casino Beaux Arts, which replaced the Huntington Bay Lodge, are shown here. In 1906, the hotel property was sold to the Bustanoby brothers, Louis, Andre, and Jacques. The Bustanobys commissioned the famous architect Sanford White to build a million-dollar casino, which he named the Beaux Arts. According to newspaper stories, it was built along the lines of the famous casino at Monte Carlo. It was said that millions of dollars changed hands across its gambling tables. The brothers renovated the hotel and renamed it the Chateau. They enlarged the bathing houses, planted lavish gardens, built a pier, and established a ferry service from Stamford, Connecticut, and a steamboat service from New York City. They even constructed underground tunnels to protect the privacy of the wealthy patrons. It was rumored that bootleg whiskey was transported through those tunnels during Prohibition. (Both, Pamela Griffin Hansen.)

Located on the main floor was a lounge large enough to entertain 1,000 guests. This magnificent area was often compared with the Hall of Mirrors at Versailles. The architects built the casino on two levels, which required cutting into the hill. The structure was at approximately the same location as the Bay Club. At that time, steamboats brought patrons from New York City to Huntington, the railroad had improved its regular service to the town, and the automobile had come on the scene. The photograph below shows the lavish interior of the dining room in the Casino Beaux Arts. (Both, Joanne Kois, Head of the Bay Club.)

The Casino Beaux Arts site is seen from two different angles. The April 1913 *Long Islander* reported a series of actions including a $250,000 damage suit filed by Jacques Bustanoby against a local resident for alienating the affections of his wife. Subsequently, the Beaux Arts Park was sold. Andre Bustanoby died in 1916, followed by his brother Louis in 1917. The morning after Louis's death, newspapers reported that a mysterious woman had telephoned the coroner's office declaring that Louis had been killed by slow poisoning. The matter never came to court, but the most colorful eight-year period in the Bay Club's glamorous history had come to an end. (Both, Joanne Kois, Head of the Bay Club.)

CASINO AND SHORE VIEW FROM CHATEAU BEAUX RIVAGE   HUNTINGTON, L. I

In 1939, the newly reorganized Huntington Crescent Club acquired the Bay Club property. The opening was held at the Beaux Arts building in the early 1940s and was attended by many prominent people, such as the president of the Crescent Club, William F. Stafford; James A. Farley, former postmaster general under Franklin D. Roosevelt; William Kissam Vanderbilt; and George B. Cortelyou, Huntington Bay Club's first president and postmaster general and secretary of commerce and labor under Theodore Roosevelt. (Huntington Historical Society.)

Huntington Yacht Club was organized on September 15, 1894, during a meeting at J.W. Shepard's home. The constitution and bylaws were adopted, and officers and trustees were elected. Henry H. Gordon was the first commodore. The entrance fee was $25, with $15 yearly dues. The club's intent was to promote sociability, create interest in yachting and aquatic sports, and provide a suitable clubhouse with anchorage for the use of its members. The bylaws provided for three regattas annually. (Henrietta Schavran.)

The hurricane of 1938 caused water to rise two and a half feet over the first floor of the yacht club's structure. Volunteers and members worked to save the club. Member Joan D'Auria, then seven years old, was carried to safety by the club manager. (Henrietta Schavran.)

On May 2, 1913, a group of 22 "motor boatmen" met at the Halesite Fire Department building to form a boating club. On May 12, they met again and formed the Ketewomoke Yacht Club of Huntington, with a charter membership of 80. The club was incorporated on June 4, 1913. Not having a clubhouse, they accepted an offer by Moses L. Scudder for the temporary use of the old Johnson homestead and dock until the club could build its own. A celebration was held on July 4, 1913, that included an 18-mile motorboat race, picnic, and fireworks display. (Oliver Bodine and John Almberg.)

A year after Ketewomoke Yacht Club's formation, its new clubhouse was completed; it now holds title to the oldest yacht club building on Long Island in continuous operation. Over the years, Ketewomoke Yacht Club included members from many old Huntington families, including famous yacht designer and builder William Atkin and Ketewomoke Yacht Club's world-renowned artist in-residence, Arthur Dove. The club is much the same as it was in 1914, retaining its comfortable "old shoe" feel with wainscot walls, original tin ceiling, and the pleasing aroma of the old wooden oar lockers. (Oliver Bodine, KYC archives.)

The 42-foot yawl Mona, purchased from silent screen star William Hart, served as a home and floating studio for Arthur Dove and his fellow painter and paramour, Helen "Reds" Torr, for seven years until, in 1929, the winter cold and the effects of paint fumes forced them to seek larger, warmer quarters. Dove offered Ketewomoke Yacht Club $15 a month if he could take up residence and have his studio on the clubhouse's second floor. The club secretary said that he could use the space for free just to have someone in the building over the winter. Today, Dove's paintings and drawings are in many of the world's finest collections and museums. In the 1960s, several of his works were discovered in the attic of Ketewomoke Yacht Club and were donated to the Heckscher Museum in Huntington. (Oliver Bodine.)

William Atkin, Andre Bustanoby, and other locals brought international motorboat races to Long Island and, for a short time, made the sleepy little town of Huntington the epicenter of motorboat racing. August Heckscher's Nameless and T.J. Chesbrough's Restless were both Atkin designs and were built at the Atkin-Wheeler shop in Halesite to compete in the 1910 Harmsworth Trophy Race, the premier international motorboat race of the time. Frederick Burnham, driving Dixie II, bested his British rival Pioneer, owned by the Duke of Westminster, winning the 1910 trophy for America. It stayed here until 1913, when it was won back by the United Kingdom. (Oliver Bodine and John Almberg.)

In 1928, Hall and Ruland distributed a prospectus and advertised in the Sunday edition of the *New York Mirror*, describing the "private bathing beaches, the $195 to $2000 bungalow lots for sale in Centerport, and the delightful setting of this incomparable summer colony." The land to be developed had been purchased from the Irwin and Fleet families and was part of the old Fleet family's original tract. (Greenlawn-Centerport Historical Association.)

In the 1930s, an open-air platform was built at Taylor Street and Washington Drive where meetings and dances were held. It was blown off its foundation by a major storm in 1951, and a new one was erected. The building, completely remodeled, is used by members of the Centerport Beach Association. The building on the left was purchased by the association in the 1960s to provide permanent restrooms for the community beach. (Greenlawn-Centerport Historical Association.)

Visit us at
arcadiapublishing.com

www.ingramcontent.com/pod-product-compliance
Lightning Source LLC
Chambersburg PA
CBHW060937170426
43194CB00027B/2983